W9-BZX-534

ANGLER'S WORKBENCH

100's of TIPS and PROJECTS FOR THE SMALL-BOAT ANGLER

By:

KEITH WALTERS

PUBLISHED BY:

AERIE HOUSE

P. O. BOX 279

BOZMAN, MD 21612-0279

BOOK DESIGN AND EDITING BY:

CAROLE WALTERS

ANGLER'S WORKBENCH
100's of TIPS and PROJECTS FOR THE SMALL-BOAT ANGLER

Copyright © 1998 by Keith Walters

All rights reserved.

First Printing

Published in the United States of America by
KEITH WALTERS LLC, AERIE HOUSE DIVISION
P.O. Box 279, Bozman, Maryland 21612-0279.

Library of Congress Number 98-93621

ISBN 0-9627039-3-1

COVER PHOTOGRAPHS:

In the red frame, the bucktail jig in my shop vise and the simple thread bobbin indicate material and tools available in any home workshop.

All of the lures in the yellow frame were handmade by myself and my friends—and are pretty doggone professional, too.

I fitted out the "tin bass boat" in the blue frame with plywood decking and inexpensive pedestal seats—again proving the message I want to convey in this book: If I can make or modify lures, boats, tackle, and trailers with simple hand tools and readily available materials, anyone can.

For my wife of 43 years,
Jean Carole Walters

For she is still,
And will ever be—

My ray of sunshine
On the cloudiest day,

My brightest beacon
In the darkest night.

ACKNOWLEDGEMENTS ───────

First and foremost, credit for this book must go to my wife, Carole. She organized many years of projects and stacks of illegible field notes. She edited the text, designed this book, and yanked me back on track whenever I went astray. She took care of all the business of producing a book while I did the writing. Without a partner like Carole, there would be no *ANGLER'S WORKBENCH* book.

Second, there are so many people who helped me along the way by sharing fishing, boat, and tackle hints and tips. C. Boyd Pfeiffer who wrote the Foreword, provided photographs and ideas for some of the projects. It would be impossible to name you all—suffice to say that if your name is in this book, I thank you for your help. If your name does not appear here, I thank you anyway. You will be in my next fishing opus, absolutely guaranteed.

Third, thanks to *CHESAPEAKE BAY MAGAZINE*, *THE FISHERMAN*, *FISHING TACKLE TRADE NEWS*, *THE MARINER*, *SALT WATER SPORTSMAN*, and *CHESAPEAKE OUTDOOR TIMES* for permission to use portions of material I originally wrote for them.

Fourth, many thanks to the Fourth Estate—the press—most particularly the other outdoor writers who have helped me every step of the way. I hope that some day, in some way I can pay it all back.

TABLE OF CONTENTS

BOAT DOCKS

TRAILERING

ANCHORING

RODS

REELS

LURES

RIGS

KNOTS

ACCESSORIES

INTRODUCTION

Every project, tip, and hint in this book is the result of problem-solving. Tackle to be stored out of the way, lures to be made more effective (we hope!), trailering aids, rod racks—you name it.

The projects are not all-encompassing, do not solve every problem on every boat or in every tacklebox. If they did, this book would be a million pages long and cost thousands of dollars. Included, however, are enough projects to keep the average angler busy for years, as they did me! Each project or idea is explained as clearly as possible, with photographs whenever possible.

Some may object to the anecdotal style; perfectionists may want nothing but the facts, man, just the facts. But, others might enjoy a slight break in the data flow to get some background about how the problem arose and how it was solved. Bear with me, since I want this to be a fun book. That's the way I write. An anecdote once in a while can't hurt.

Take your time and select the ideas that appeal or apply to you or your situation. And, most of all, be careful!

● ● ● ● ● ● ● ● ● ● ● ● ● ● ● ●

SAFETY FIRST!!

Safety is the most important thing to remember as you do any of the projects in this, or any, book. Use common sense.

It is assumed the reader has some skills in working with common hand tools, and will exercise utmost care in keeping all body parts away from saws, drills, and other tools that, by themselves, can't tell wood, plastics, or metal from your flesh.

Never, ever, work around the water with electric power tools like drills and saws! My solution to the problem of possible electric shock is to use battery-powered tools where I can, and air-powered tools if necessary. It is a pain to drag my air compressor to the dock, and use a heavy extension cord to power it, but it would be a lot worse pain to get an electric shock. The air compressor is unplugged and rolled out on the dock until it needs more air, then I roll it back to its GFCI (Ground Fault Circuit Interrupter) breaker for a recharge. On the dock, I have a long air hose to reach the work. (See your electrician for a GFCI breaker installation—it could save you from getting shocked!).

Another way to avoid electric shock is to work on the boat on its trailer in your dry driveway. Larger boats can be modified at the boatyard before putting them in the water. Complicated modifications should be left to the experts.

Small items should be clamped to the workbench or gripped in a vise before drilling or sawing. I see pictures of people drilling sharp pieces of metal like spinnerbait blades while holding the part in their hands, and it gives me the willies. If the drill bit binds, a piece of unclamped metal becomes a rapidly-spinning meat slicer—it can puree your hand in a heartbeat!

Look behind or under the work before sawing or drilling. A sabre saw cuts a lot deeper than you think. It is possible to cut through a bulkhead, and the pipe or wires behind it, in the blink of an eye.

Pouring lead into molds to make sinkers and jigs can be dangerous. Always wear heavy leather gloves and use thick kitchen potholders when handling hot lead molds. Always work in a well-ventilated area when melting lead—it can be toxic. Occasionally I melt old tire weights for sinkers (though softer lead is recommended) and pieces of rubber tire sometimes adhere to the weight. The smell of burning rubber in a lead pot will remind you to open all windows and doors in a hurry! Always be careful when pouring into molds. A pocketful of hot lead is nothing to sneeze at!

Working with tools should always be dictated by using common sense. If something can go wrong, it will—often with disastrous results. Be careful!

"Measure twice, cut once" is an old carpenter's saw. Believe it.

Think the project through at least twice and determine if there is anything that could hurt you, then take all the necessary steps to avoid the safety hazards before you proceed with the work. You'll save time, material, and possibly bandages. Take it from me.

FOREWORD ─────────────────

One of the marks of an excellent fisherman is an inquisitive nature along with both a desire and dedication to constantly find better ways to make fishing easier through various tips, projects, ideas and modifications of tackle, boats, and accessory equipment.

Keith Walters is one of those expert anglers in both fresh and saltwater who is never satisfied with the status quo and who is always searching for ways to make fishing more efficient.

Fortunately for the rest of us, Keith has decided to put the best of the tips, projects, and ideas he has developed, found, tried and used through the years into this book. In short, it is the culmination of the best tips from years of experience by the experts. I say experts advisedly, since Keith would be the first to admit that all of these ideas are not his, although he is responsible for most of them. The important thing is they are the result of his constantly seeking better ideas for trailering, boating, tackle storage, tackle use, working with accessories, and making simple rigs for all kinds of fishing.

The book is divided into sections that together with a table of contents makes it easy to quickly find the tip or project you need to solve a problem. Want an idea on mini-outriggers for your boat, fishing tool caddies, tackle storage lockers, marine radio installation, parallel boat docking, launch ramp safety chocks, reel protectors, rod repairs, lure modifications, leader tips, various bait rigs, or pier tackle carts? It's all here.

This is a book that will save you money while making fishing more fun. Just one or two of the hundreds of tips will pay for the cost of this book—save you money on a fishing project while making fishing easier, safer, and more efficient. Enjoy, learn, and benefit from the information packed in these pages

C. Boyd Pfeiffer
Phoenix, MD
September, 1998

MY FISHING BOATS

As we mature, our view of what makes a good fishing boat changes. Youngsters who consider themselves immortal, rate the principle criteria for their ideal fishing craft thus:

1. Fishability
2. Comfort
3. Safety

At my age, I reverse the above order to: Safety, comfort, and fishability. This makes more sense, since one must be safe and comfortable to live long enough to enjoy the fishing.

Forty years ago, my first fishing boat was a 12-foot Starcraft aluminum hull powered by a 12 hp Evinrude. I've run OMC motors (Johnson or Evinrude) ever since.

My second fishing craft was a 16-foot Boston Whaler with a 40 hp Montgomery Ward by Evinrude. I had the Whaler 10 years and six motors before a dry ride became paramount.

Next, a 20-foot Mako center console with a 140 hp Johnson kept me drier in rough seas. I had the Mako 18 years and seven motors.

Then I bought a 22-foot Horizon by Angler. Aside from some gel coat stress cracks the hull has served me well. It is powered by a 175 hp Johnson FICHT.

I recently sold the 14-foot aluminum jon boat with a 15 hp Johnson described in the next chapter.

The reason I have included this progression of boats is to orient the reader, since many of the following ideas may not be in the same order as the above chronologically.

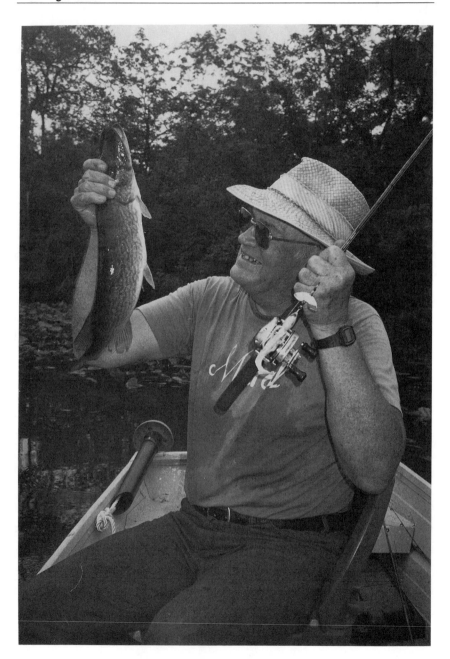

Jack Stovall shows off his "tin boat" pickerel.

BOAT PROJECTS ——————— 3

A SKINNY WATER BASS BOAT

The small aluminum bass boat has many friends. There are as many reasons for owning one as there are anglers.

For some, it's an inexpensive starter boat, for others it is a way of getting back to basic fishing after experiencing—and owning—big boats. In my case, a neighbor gave me a badly dented 14-foot Wards aluminum jon boat. The rivets leaked and he had replaced them with regular steel nuts and bolts. The oarlocks were worn out. Never look a gift horse in the mouth, or a gift boat in the rivets. A few dollars for a few accessories and I'd have a neat bass boat.

"It leaks a little," my friend warned me. No, it leaked a lot. The regular steel nuts and bolts he used to stop rivet leaks do not take kindly to saltwater, and that's what we have here in Chesapeake Bay, water salty enough to rust plastic. I replaced the regular steel nuts and bolts with stainless steel ones, caulking around them with marine silicone. I had to use 1/4-inch diameter replacement bolts, since my benefactor had already drilled out the old rivet holes, and I couldn't find 1/4-inch diameter aluminum rivets.

To check for leaks, I placed the boat upright on saw horses and half filled it with water with a garden hose and left it there for a day. A.O.K. No leaks!

Copying a friend's bassin' jon boat, I installed plywood flooring fore and aft to anchor the seats and provide a flat deck to walk on. Stumbling over crosswise ribs is uncomfortable and dangerous.

Preferring comfort while casting for bass all day, I installed inexpensive folding seats, one for the forward angler, and one aft for the captain. None of those slim bicycle seat-leaning posts for me. My back tires too quickly.

Two cardboard templates were made, one between the front crosswise seat and the bow, and one for the space between the middle and aft crosswise seats. Since the bow of a jon boat sweeps up somewhat, I made several shallow saw cuts (kerfs) across the underside of the front decking plywood, so I could easily bend it to fit the upward curve of the tin.

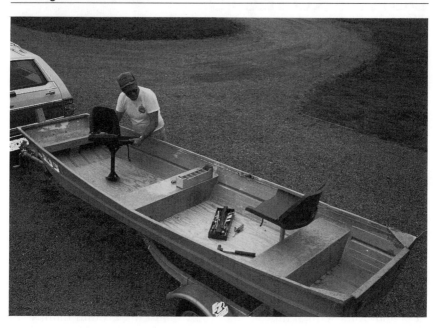

The author installing swivel seats in the tin boat.

When the plywood fit the floor, the position of the raised aluminum crosswise floor braces was scribed on the plywood and marked with a chalk line. I measured the maximum depth I could drill into the raised ribs, then subtracted a little so I wouldn't drill through the boat's bottom, then marked the depth on the drill bit with tape. I wanted to drill through plywood and just one thickness of aluminum. The second thickness of aluminum is the bottom. The drill bit was slightly smaller than the diameter of the short Phillips stainless self-tapping tapered head screws I used to anchor the plywood floor. Tapered washers were used to keep the screws from digging too deeply into the plywood.

If I had it to do over again, I would use Quadraplex, or square drive stainless steel screws. Phillips head screws get buggered up too easily with repeated use. The flooring and seats are removed for out-of-the-weather storage each winter and put back in the boat in the spring.

The tin boat rigged out for bass fishing with electric and outboard motors.

A mushroom anchor fit nicely into the end of a piece of plastic pipe secured near the bow as shown in photo above. The anchor line leads back along the gunwale to a cleat near the rear seat. On the fishing grounds, the anchor dangles from the pipe. While trailering, it is secured in its pipe holder.

Mounting a front electric trolling motor was simple. I fitted an angled block of wood inside the bow so the motor would clamp to a flat surface. I loosened a screw and rotated the tube on the electric motor so both the hand control and propeller faced aft.

I've had second thoughts about a front-mount electric motor. On a bass guide's boat, the captain sits in the front and steers the boat. He gets first shot at the water with his lures. The paying customer gets the second shot at the water. Guide Perry Munro in Nova Scotia mounted his trolling motor on the stern. I got *first shot* at all those neat little fish hidey-holes. Munro pointed me right at them from his position at the stern. He got second shot at the water—and he caught more fish, on a fly rod yet, but that's another story.

Mounting a new 15 hp Johnson was easy. I simply hung it on, drilled two 1/4" holes through the transom for stainless steel bolts that go through the motor bracket and somewhat permanently secure the motor to the hull. Then I buggered the bolt threads to make it more entertaining for thieves. A motor lock over the clamp screw handles may also slow down potential crooks. Portable items are removed whenever the boat is not in use.

A galvanized trailer pretty much completed my rig, except for some niceties like an old-style flasher depth finder. I chose a galvanized trailer because I often fish shallow saltwater creeks with the tin boat. The trailer dealer mounted a 2" ball coupling on my trailer to be compatible with my big boat trailer. Now, I don't have to change hitch balls to tow different boats.

The tin boat has allowed me to fish Maryland's really skinny waters, like the Tuckahoe River for pickerel, creeks off the upper Choptank for white perch and bass, the Marshyhope (tough pick for bass), and my favorite bass river, the Pocomoke above Snow Hill.

My tin boat "gift" was not cost free. A new 15 hp Johnson outboard motor, a small electric trolling motor, trailer, plywood, seats, and other accessories were necessities. I figure I have about $1500 in the rig—not a bad price for such a versatile backwater boat, though it would have been cheaper if I'd shopped for a used motor and trailer.

Some offshore anglers are returning to their small-boat roots. A friend recently bought an offshore boat so he could chase after tuna and billfish more comfortably. Where does he spend most of his time? In a 16-foot tin boat, banging around stumps and rocks chasing sea trout and stripers. Go figure.

PITCHFORK PROPELLER PROTECTOR

Anglers who fish in rocky rivers like the Susquehanna in the upper Chesapeake Bay justifiably worry about their propellers.

Outdoor writer C. Boyd Pfeiffer solved that problem by attaching a pitchfork in front of his propeller. You may see a lot of these rigs on small boats on the Susquehanna and many other rocky rivers.

Some welding was required. A piece of bar stock with appropriately spaced holes replaced the round tube that accepted the pitchfork's original wooden handle. Then four pieces of flat steel stock were cut to a length which would wrap around the lower

Photo by C. Boyd Pfeiffer

unit (two on either side) of Boyd's outboard motor a few inches above the cavitation plate. Never block your motor's water intakes! The steel straps were fastened with stainless steel round head bolts, washers, and Nylock nuts.

A few wraps of electrician's tape around the tines closest to the propeller shaft's torpedo-shaped housing protects the housing from excessive abuse.

When the motor is in forward gear, the tilt control is left in the kick-up position so it will ride over rocks in the shallows. The steel straps can be painted, but if they finally rust, they are easily replaced. Outboard motors equipped with a pitchfork prop protector might not be as efficient, but their propellers last a lot longer!

• • • • • • • • • • • • • • • •

OAR STORAGE ON A TIN BOAT

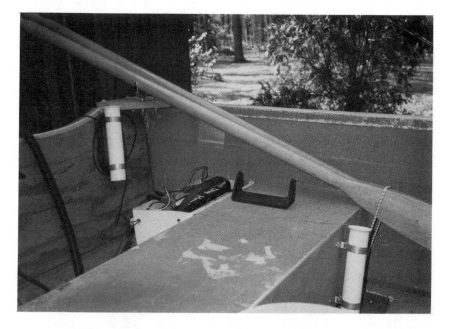

To keep his oars out of the way and secure while trailering, Jim Walker drilled two holes in the horizontal brace to accommodate his oarlock pins. The blades of the oars are secured with bungee cord.

HANDY TIN BOAT ROD REST

Fishing rods are always in the way in small boats, increasing the possibility of damage to expensive equipment, and also increasing the possibility that someone will trip over loose gear.

C. Boyd Pfeiffer protects his rod tips with PVC pipe or golf club tubes secured to the bulkhead of his jon boat. A piece of wood shaped to hold the handles is secured to the aft seat, with bungee cord tie-downs.

Photo by C. Boyd Pfeiffer

Pfeiffer's rods are kept separated and out of harm's way.

PUSH POLE

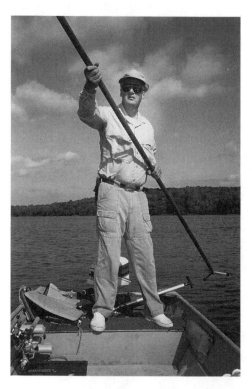

C. Boyd Pfeiffer made his own push pole from a 14-foot length of fiberglass rod made for that purpose. One end is pointed. At the opposite end Boyd added a spring-loaded "duck bill" that splays out when the pole is pushed against the water and retracts when it is retrieved for the next push.

Boyd suggests that a 14-, 15-, or 16-foot piece of closet rod is cheaper and would serve the same purpose if properly treated. Duck bills can be purchased from mail order catalogs, and closet rod to fit the duck bill's diameter is available at most lumber yards.

You must make sure your pole is straight and has no snags or splinters that would snag your hands. He suggests two or more coats of varnish after a good sanding.

Boyd made three sideways "U" brackets to hold his push pole. The center one faced opposite from the front and rear ones. But, fiberglass is less likely to take a set than closet rod, so a pole made from wood should be stored inside when not in use.

A 12-foot aluminum telescoping boat hook might appeal to some as a shallow water push pole, but it could get hung up in rocky bottom and pull you overboard, or come in contact with an underwater electrical cable—bad idea! For the same expense you could make one of fiberglass.

PUSH POLE CLAMPS

Push poles are handy to have when you don't want to run a gas or electric motor in shallow water, but a 16-foot pole can be hard to store on a 14-foot boat.

C. Boyd Pfeiffer's solution was to store the pole on the hull's exterior. Two U-shaped clamps were installed, fore and aft, with the open part of the "U" facing upward. An L-shaped clamp was installed amidships, with a slight turned-down lip at the outside end to hold the pole in place, yet make it easy to remove for use. The center clamp was covered with a piece of plastic hose to prevent abrasion to the pole.

Photo by C. Boyd Pfeiffer

MORE TIN BOAT TIPS

• Make a cheap small-boat anchor by filling a large #10 tin can with cement. Put an eye bolt in the concrete before it sets up.

• Mount a sailboat cam cleat on the bow that will accept your anchor line. Then, mount a regular cleat near the rear seat, handy to the helmsman. Thread your anchor rode through the cam cleat and string it back to the helm through two or three plastic pipe brackets along the gunwales. Hang the anchor off the bow, lower it by giving a tug on the rode to free the cam cleat and drop the anchor. Secure the anchor rode on the rear cleat. See photo on page 105.

• When spray painting a skiff for extra use as a duck boat, first give the craft a background-color base coat. Check with your paint dealer for proper colors for your area. When the base coat dries, cut some leaf-bearing tree limbs and hold them next to the base coat as you spray the contrasting color. The leaf patterns will give a random camouflage look. Some say fish are not as easily spooked by camo-painted boats in the shallows.

• When making a drag chain on a short rode to slow your drift, make sure the rode is not long enough to reach the motor's propeller! This limits the drag chain for use in shallow water only. With a short rode, it is not necessary to pick up the drag chain every time you move for another drift. See page 103 also.

• Tin boat trailers with side or bottom bunks to guide the boat on can be made "slicker" by replacing the carpet with 1/4-inch thick polyethylene board. Attach it to the wood bunks with countersunk stainless steel screws to keep from scratching the boat hull. Poly helps the boat slide effortlessly, making retrieval easier.

• Cartoppers need to tie their boats securely to the vehicle. Boyd Pfeiffer drilled one hole in the top of his front bumper, and two holes in the top of his rear bumper for eyebolts. His tie-down ropes were terminated with S-hooks and a spring-loaded levered latch from a boat-trailer store took up the slack. His roof rack was made of 1 x 2 in. laths. I suggested a bracket at the top rear of the car's roof rack that would be a roller—a piece of PVC pipe over a galvanized pipe, perhaps.

• Make your own jon boat trailer guide-ons as shown above from PVC pipe. Mine was made from one-inch i.d. PVC pipe, two 90-degree elbows, and two end caps. The U-shaped assembly was attached to the rear crossbrace of the trailer by drilling 5/16-inch holes through the pipe and the trailer frame for 1/4-inch stainless steel bolts capped with Nylock nuts with stainless steel washers under the nuts. One could also use stainless steel or plated steel U-bolts if the trailer frame permits. The PVC pipe is about eight inches higher than the boat gunwale, allowing the vehicle operator to back the trailer down the ramp easier. The PVC assembly is about four inches wider than the hull. Some boaters use larger diameter PVC pipe and mount their tail lights at the top of the pipe ends for greater visibility. This also keeps the lights out of the water at the launch ramp.

• Plywood decking is a lot safer and more comfortable in a tin boat than the aluminum reinforcement ribs that are easy to trip over, and hard on the feet. Even better, some say, is outdoor carpeting on the plywood.

- Duck hunters might also cover their aluminum seats with carpet to protect their shotguns.
- Use an old piece of carpet under the gas tank to cut down on metal-to-metal noise.
- Boyd Pfeiffer uses an old outboard motor gas tank hose as a manual bilge pump. He removed the motor connectors from both ends of the hose, placed the suction end in the bilge, and the motor end overboard. The squeeze bulb is placed on the floor near the operator, who simply presses on it with his foot to pump the bilge.

● ● ● ● ● ● ● ● ● ● ● ● ● ● ● ●

ROD HOLDER BAITBOARD

An inexpensive, easily-stored rod-holder baitboard can quickly be made in the home shop. Readily-available parts include a 1-1/2 inch o.d. chrome-plated brass sink drain tailpipe 12 inches long, a piece of scrap plywood (mine is 9 x 15 inches), and several stainless steel screws shorter than the plywood is thick.

A 12-inch piece of chrome-plated brass sink tailpipe I already had was just the right diameter to fit snugly in my gunwale rod holders. To get a mark as level as possible, I measured when the boat was in the water. I put the pipe into the rod holder, held a level near the top, and drew a "level" line with a permanent black marker. Then I continued that line all the way around the pipe, and circumscribed another line about an inch below that.

In the shop, I hacksawed off one end of the pipe at the top "level" line, then cut six tabs, approximately one-inch by one inch each, down to the lower "level" line with a pair of tin snips.

Next the tabs were bent and flattened (see top photo on opposite page) so the pipe would support the plywood roughly level when the baitboard was placed in the rod holder. Holes were drilled in each tab. Pencil lines drawn from corner to corner on the bottom of the plywood found the board's center, where the pipe was screwed to the baitboard with screws too short to penetrate the plywood.

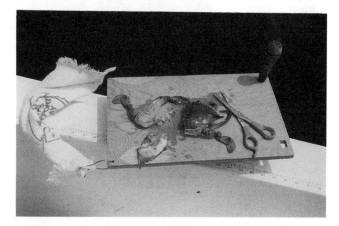

After positioning the baitboard in a rod holder, I marked and cut slots in the bottom of the pipe to fit the rod holder's gimbal pins. A slight outboard slant will allow bait juices to drip overboard. Two slots hold a filet knife and an inexpensive pair of stainless steel scissors (see lower photo above) I use to cut fragile baits like squid or soft crabs. When the plywood or other scrap board gets too rough looking, simply replace it with another piece of scrap lumber.

A fancier baitboard can be made by substituting a polyethylene cutting board from the local kitchen store.

Two cautions: (1) Make sure the pipe fits into your rod holder snugly to hold it steady, and (2) Use short screws that don't protrude to the cutting surface or you'll dull a lot of knives.

SINK CUTOUT BAITBOARD

Another handy bait-cutting board for your boat can be easily made from the plastic laminate-covered countertop cutout left over when a kitchen cabinet craftsman installs a kitchen sink. A plywood backing will hold up longer in the wet boating environment than the flakeboard material usually used for kitchen countertops.

Omar Stoltzfus cleans a king mackerel on the baitboard.

Kitchen cabinet installers usually have the cutouts lying around the shop and are happy to give them away—although a six-pack of beverages would make a thoughtful trade. Most cutouts will have a pilot hole drilled near one corner to start the saber-saw blade. I turned my sink cutout over and laid out a nice rectangle on the backside with a carpenter's square and a pencil that excluded the drilled hole. An electric hand saw with a plywood blade made a neat cut with the laminate face down. A small pilot hole was drilled for a saber saw cut to hold the bait knife.

The baitboard can then be laid on an I/O engine box as is, or various devices can be attached to the back of the board to adapt it to your individual boat. To fit my Mako splashwell, I glued two pieces of 2 x 4 to the underside of the baitboard far enough apart so they would fit neatly on each side of the splashwell wall.

When not in use, I store the baitboard along the side of the boat, held in place by a piece of shock cord. The plastic laminate on my baitboard is easy to clean, doesn't seem to dull the bait knife, and will outlast the backing board.

• • • • • • • • • • • • • • •

MINI-OUTRIGGERS

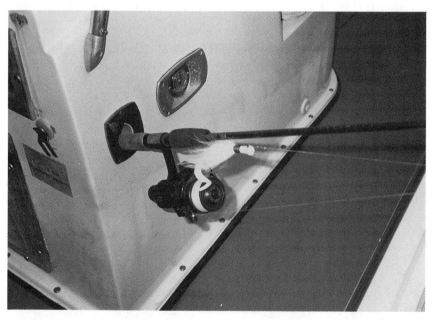

Shallow-water trolling from a center console boat can be enhanced by adding standard flush-mount gunwhale rod holders horizontally in the sides of the boat's console. Normally, these rod holders are mounted vertically in the gunwhale tops, and hold fishing rods at a slight backwards angle. But, rods can be held out horizontally like mini-outriggers when the holders are mounted as in the photographs.

When trolling in shallow water, one assumes any fish under the boat scoot away to avoid the boat and its propeller. These mini-outriggers place the rod tip and the line well outside the sides of the boat hull. Naturally, the longer the rod, the farther out the rod tips will be. Hopefully, trolling lures to the side, and behind the boat 100 feet or more, places the baits where the fish have stopped to admire the departing boat and will resume feeding. Trolling with 10-foot surf rods in the mini-riggers in 10 feet of water down-current from Chesapeake Bay Bridge pilings with 14-inch long Creek Chub swimming plugs, we often caught stripers to 30 pounds.

In my home river, Maryland's Choptank, locals troll in water so shallow their outboard motor lower units bang over rocks. Placing trolling rods upright in gunwhale holders places the baits behind the boat right in the propwash. Getting lures out to the side is more productive.

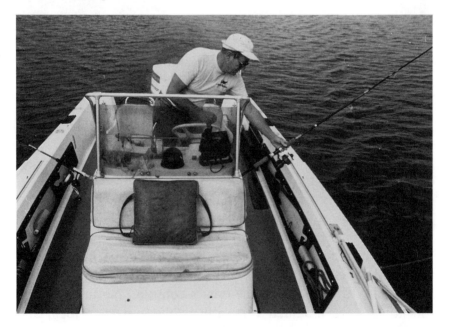

I once tried regular outriggers in these shallows (and got some funny sideways glances from passing locals), but the slack in the outrigger lines made it almost impossible to hook striking fish.

Offshore, where a dropback might be necessary, some slack might be desirable. In shallow water, slack line assures missed strikes. With these mini-outriggers, there is no slack in the line, and a striking fish is easily hooked.

Lures used with mini-outriggers must run shallow and not dig down like deep swimming plugs. In shallow water, 1/4-oz. bucktails decorated with a piece of ripple rind or a swimmertail grub will "float" above the bottom far enough to keep from snagging.

We have also successfully trolled regular surface popping plugs in our mini-outriggers to locate schools of blues and stripers, then we stopped and cast to them with lighter tackle.

● ● ● ● ● ● ● ● ● ● ● ● ● ●

DOWNRIGGERS

Downriggers on my 20-foot Mako allowed us to troll lures 30 to 50 feet deep with 14 pound-test spinning tackle. Bluefish caught on downriggers sometimes blew out of the water and jumped across the surface like miniature tarpon.

Great Lakes trollers get even more excitement by "stacking" several fishing lines vertically on each downrigger line, but we found one angler per downrigger line was more than enough when good numbers of hungry fish were present.

I mounted two Penn 600 downriggers, one unit on each side of my Mako's motor well at the transom, pointing straight aft. The downrigger's two foot arm kept the cable well behind the outboard's propeller. These units have crank-operated reels with 200 feet of cable, a footage counter, a brake that pays out cable in case the weight hangs up on bottom, and a ball-shaped weight with a built-in line release.

Later, I moved the downriggers amidships so we wouldn't have to hang out two feet behind the transom to reconnect our lines to downrigger balls. Now they are mounted on the gunwhales about six feet ahead of the transom with the booms pointed outward. They are much easier to operate in that location. A swivel downrigger mount would be even handier.

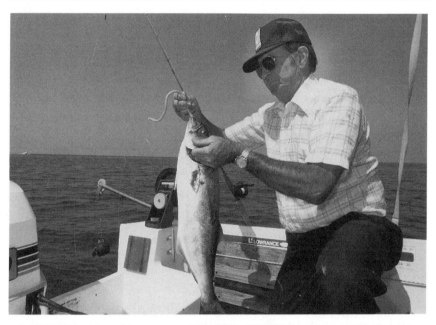

Jack Wiley with a "downrigger" bluefish. Downriggers were on the stern.

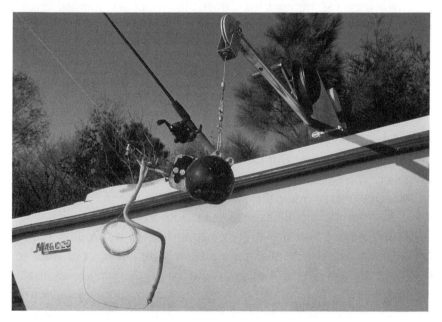

Downriggers mounted amidships for handier access.

With a 10-pound weight on each cable, I rig up leaders and lures. Surgical hose lures and spoons should oscillate or swim to be effective, but they sometimes spin and twist a leader. A ball bearing snap swivel between the release tab on the downrigger ball and the hose lure prevents leader twist. The reel's line is tied to the swivel eye next to the release on the downrigger ball. Fifteen feet of 30-pound test leader between the hose lure at the business end and the ball bearing swivel completes the rig.

Put spinning or levelwind bass-size outfits in rod holders, set reel drags loose enough to peel off line, then lower the downrigger weights to where the depthfinder marked fish. Then, retighten the reel drag on light bass or spinning outfits so there is a lot of bend in the rod, and replace rods in the holders. A big bend in the fishing rod will snatch the slack out of the line when the fish hits.

Depthfinders with wide angle (45 degree) transducers will show downrigger weights on the screen. My narrow 20 degree-angle transducer does not. With no bites after several passes, raise the downrigger weights in five-foot increments until you get in the strike zone. Most fish rise up to hit lures several feet above their line of vision instead of at their eye level.

Anglers who are skilled machinists like Bob Prince can make their own downriggers. Bob machined the reel and arm for the downrigger assembly shown in the photo on the left. He also made a mold for the downrigger weight, and included a stabilizer fin when he poured it. I mounted the base of the unit to a teak step pad on my Mako by removing the pad and recessing four stainless steel 1/4-20 nuts in the bottom of the teak block. Next, four 1/4-20 screws attached the downrigger to the step pad.

Downrigger accessories include: Remotely-controlled electric motors, rod holders, swivel mounts, "scent-rigger" weights that you can pack with chum, flashy prism attractors, speed and temperature readouts, dash panel electronic depth indicators, and a transom mounting bracket that holds up to four downrigger reels, to name but a few.   You can stack four or more lines on each vertical downrigger line by adding release clips at intervals.

To try this type of fishing at little cost, simply hang a downrigger ball or sash weight overboard with a line release at the weight; tie it to a piece of clothesline marked every ten feet with a black Sharpie®. Any way you do it, you can double your light-tackle fishing fun with downriggers.

TIP: An extra pair of downrigger mount bases and some open space on the garage ceiling combine to make a good place to hang hard-to-store downriggers.

⚠ For safety, make sure the mounting screws for the extra bases go far enough into the ceiling **joists** so they won't pull out!

• • • • • • • • • • • • • • •

HANDY CHART PROTECTORS

Keeping charts available near the helm and out of the weather is always a problem on fishing boats. For years I kept navigation charts in the zipper-locked clear plastic envelopes sold for that purpose in stationery stores. Chart books fit in the envelopes—even the larger NOAA charts will fit when folded to show the intended fishing area.

To keep charts handy and visible when navigating in bad weather in my first center console boats, I stretched bungee cord across the lower windshield, which blocked part of my view when I sat down to steer the boat. I soon found that a horizontal surface was best for the chart protectors, but they needed to be secured to keep them from blowing away or tumbling to the deck in a bouncing boat. Again, bungee cord was the handiest way to secure the charts.

On my 22 foot walk-around cuddy cabin boat, there is a handy place on top of the hinged cabin hatch that will accommodate two chart envelopes (see photo above). One of my two envelopes holds a local chart. The other plastic pocket displays both a tide chart and the Loran-C waypoints of my favorite fishing hot spots.

These envelopes are again held in place with bungee cord. I drilled a small hole in the vertical lip on each side of the cabin hatch door to accommodate the bungee cord, tied a simple double overhand knot on the inside, and stretched the cord tight.

The only problem is a transfer of computer or copier print to the inside of the plastic envelope, so everything must be changed at least annually. But, plastic envelopes are inexpensive, and my Loran-C waypoints change almost as frequently as the tides. The advantage of this system is a clear, weatherproof spot handy to the helm.

TACKLE STORAGE LOCKERS

After years of tripping over tackle boxes on boat decks, I finally solved the problem. By combining the empty space inside the raised fiberglass pedestal under the seats of my 22-foot walk-around cuddy boat with plastic storage boxes I created out-of-the-way tackle storage. An additional benefit is the plastic boxes can be easily changed with the seasons and available fishing.

There are several ready-made tackle storage systems on the market, but none fit the space I had, or my budget. My system is based on inexpensive Plano #3700 StowAway plastic boxes with snap-closing lids, one box for each type of lure (spoon, plug, jig and grub, bucktail, etc.).

The #3700 box would only fit lengthwise into the space I had available. There was room for four plastic lure boxes under each seat, for a total of eight boxes at one time. For different species of fish, I simply exchange the boxes in the boat with others stored in the garage. In addition, I keep four extra lure boxes in a Plano #1296 carrier in the boat's cabin.

To make sure there were no obstructions under the seats, I first cut a six-inch diameter inspection hole with a sabre saw. If there were any problems at this point, I could have installed a round inspection port and cancelled the project. There were no interior obstructions, so I continued. (See photo on page 24).

I built two wooden crates, or lockers, of 5/16-inch marine plywood, each with three shelves. Each locker accommodates four #3700 boxes. Inside dimensions of the lockers are 9-1/2 inches square and 14-3/8 inches deep. Spacing is 2-1/8 inches between shelves, since #3700 boxes are 2 inches high. Dado cuts 1/8-inch deep in the sides of the lockers accommodate the 12-3/4 inch long shelves. This allows enough overhang to grasp the 14-inch long #3700 boxes. (See photo above).

Shelves are held in place with 3-penny finishing nails and epoxy. The lockers are painted with two coats of West System epoxy.

After cutting a 10-1/4 inch square opening (slightly larger than the outside dimension of my lockers) under each seat, I attached 2 x 2 in. hardwood cleats like a "picture frame" around the inside of the openings with epoxy and 1-1/2 inch stainless steel #2 square-drive flat head screws. Again, screw holes were pre-drilled.

Next, the lockers were flush-mounted inside the opening and secured with 1-1/2 inch flat head stainless steel #2 square-drive screws to the inside cleat. One of the mounting screws from the seat above was removed and replaced with a longer bolt that mated with a t-nut in the top rear of the locker for additional

support. Clear silicone sealer was applied where the lockers met the bulkheads, and stock 12 x 12 in. louvered teak doors purchased from a marine supply store were made ready to mount. First, I milled off the raised lip inside the door frame with a dado blade on my radial arm saw so it would mount flush. The doors were joined to their frames with stainless steel offset cabinet hinges and plastic door catches.

The doors and frame units were attached to the bulkhead outside the lockers with 1 inch long #1 square-drive stainless steel flat head trim screws (see photograph on page 27). Edges were sealed with clear silicone.

Tackle storage units were attached to the bulkhead.

Finally, plastic insect screen was stapled to the inside of the louvered teak doors to keep out tiny critters.

My smoke-colored #3700 Plano boxes were labelled with a Sharpie waterproof pen on yellow waterproof tape. The newer #3700 boxes are translucent white so you can see your lures better, and the Sharpie pen shows up well on them without using the yellow tape.

The advantages are flexibility, portability, and out-of-the way storage that lessens the danger of tripping over a tackle box.

TIP: I used Comet® cleanser to remove layout lines and scuff marks from the fiberglass.

PIPE STRUCTURES ON FISHING BOATS

All manner of lightweight structures have been added to boats to raise the angler's point of view or hold various accessories like lights, provide leaning posts, and in one case of one disabled angler, a custom-made pipe support to surround and support him so he can cast from the front deck.

Your boat manufacturer or dealer can direct you to a tower fabricator in your neighborhood. Some of the largest tower makers have mockups and dimensions of most popular boats so they can ship you a custom tower or platform and your local dealer can install it.

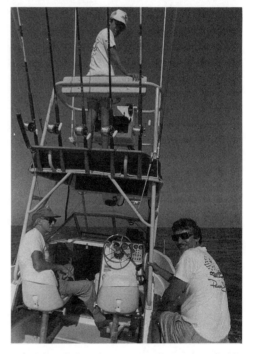

While it is probably best to have a custom welding shop fabricate a pipe tower or rear poling platform, a skilled welder can make his own rig. Tom Seiler of Port Charlotte, Florida is a skilled welder, so he made his own aluminum pipe "Tarpon Tower" to give him long-range visibility. He would have made it of stainless steel tubing, but he had previously sold his MIG welder. The Tarpon Hunters Club he belongs to "hunts" tarpon schools with several similarly equipped boats, and when they find a school, they surround it, drop anchor, and fish with dead baits. They are very successful, too, judging by the trip I took with him.

Brian Seiler scans the Gulf of Mexico for tarpon from the tuna tower while his father Tom (right) and the late Bill Perry play a waiting game in the tarpon hunt.

Sherman Baynard stands on his push-pole platform.

Sherman Baynard of Centreville, MD installed a removeable push-pole platform for his 17-foot Mako, making his vessel one of the best shallow-water "flats boats" I've seen. He also removed the bow rail and two seats behind the console, giving him plenty of room to fly- or spin-cast lures in Chesapeake shallows.

The upside-down "U" made of stainless steel pipe in this chapter used for safety grab handles could be fabricated much larger and used for a back brace when fly-fishing all day. Flush sockets for the pipe could be let into the front deck wherever convenient, and the U-brace removed whenever necessary.

Dr. Ed Hahn built a PVC pipe rack to hold his extremely bright night fishing lights 10 feet above the water as required in Delaware Bay. He powers them with a small portable generator. There are so many more uses of PVC pipe on board boats: It can be cut to length and used for rod holders all over the boat, including those attached to bow rails with stainless steel hose clamps, or fastened to bulkheads with screws or nuts and bolts. A slot can be cut in the top to accommodate spinning rod or levelwind reel seats—or cut even deeper to allow for fly reel seats.

MD DNR biologist, Ben Florence (left), and Dr. Reggie Harrell of the University of MD's Horn Point Lab bring in a spawning striper.

The Maryland DNR's 25-foot "chase boat" is used to pick up huge spawning striped bass cows after they were electro-shocked by another boat. A large tank on board is filled with saltwater and tranquilizer so the females can be calmed while in transport to the hatchery where they are spawned out. Many times the boats are used at night, hence the lights on a PVC pipe rack that anyone could easily fabricate to their own specifications. Do not depend on PVC pipe to support people, since it can break under less stress than the stainless steel or aluminum pipe structures mentioned earlier.

A HANDY TOOL CADDY

Finding the right pair of pliers or a hook disgorger when fishing is "hot" can be a problem. Murphy's Law says whatever you need most in a hurry will be hardest to find.

To solve this problem, I first looked for the location closest to most of my fishing. On my previous center console boat, it was the back of the seats. On my present walk-around cuddy cabin boat the seatbacks are again close to the action.

The rest of the job was simple:

• I cut a length of old leather belt that would span the two vertical cushion straps on the seatback, and wrapped the belt around both straps to form loops.

• Loops were closed with snaps, but pop rivets (even nuts and bolts), would serve the same purpose.

• Plier and knife sheaths were threaded on the "belt," and I was able to hang "hook-outers" on the belt, too.

My seatback tool caddy is not only handy to the fishing, it keeps knives and pliers in one spot and safely off the deck.

HARD-SIDED TOOL CADDY

C. Boyd Pfeiffer made this hard-sided tool caddy for his fiberglass boat some years ago. He was concerned that leather sheaths like the previous rig that I made might expose knife blades and "filet someone" as he explained it.

Photo by C. Boyd Pfeiffer

As shown in the photograph on the left, the caddy is made from several layers of plywood with a layer of plexiglass between tools for visibility. The caddy is bolted together and mounted to a vertical bulkhead.

Boyd simply placed each tool on a piece of plywood and traced around it, then cut the wood around the outline with a sabre saw. Thicker tools required two layers of plywood.

The plexiglass and the plywood layers were cut shorter than the tools so their handles could be reached easily. Stainless steel bolts, washers, and nuts could be used for assembly, and through-bolted to a bulkhead. Also short stainless steel screws could be used to assemble the unit, with longer ones in the center to mount it to a bulkhead.

Tools included fishing pliers, a leader crimper, screwdriver, hook file, bait knife, and a filet knife. The layout could include any tool that would be handy on your boat.

Though Boyd used plywood layers painted white, one could also use polyethylene cutting board for the layers of opaque material. Use a fine tooth, hollow ground planer saw blade to get a nice smooth cut. Shape the unit to fit the space available.

Clean your tools before replacing them in the caddy, or fish slime could give the unit an unpleasant odor in a short time.

• • • • • • • • • • • • • • •

CONVENIENT LURE KEEPERS

Most of us have several favorite lures we use on a continuing basis. Rooting around in a tackle box when we want to change a lure is out of the question. Takes too long when the fish are biting.

For years, I used a piece of bungee cord stretched crossways behind my center console windshield. The large saltwater poppers we used then were hung by their tail hooks. In recent years, we use smaller lures, bucktails, knife-handle spoons, and single-hook plugs that have been converted from baits that came with two trebles.

Sherman Baynard wrapped a piece of foam pipe insulation around the grab rail on his center console, and secured it with stainless steel hose clamps. Nylon cable ties could also be used. Sherman's favorite small bucktail jigs are always handy right in front of the steering station. Bass anglers also use pipe insulation attached to the pedestal of a bass boat seat to keep lures in use handy. The same insulation is used around the outside rail of a pipe T-top as a fly rod cushion for rods stored vertically alongside the center console, and could save a delicate rod for a wild caster.

Sherman Baynard's foam pipe insulation around the grab rail of his center console boat to hold his lures.

A foam plastic fly box I won at a fishing fundraiser works great as a handy temporary lure keeper.

Lures with treble hooks go inside the hinged fly box, and single-hook baits like bucktail jigs are simply stuck in the sides of the box. A piece of fairly dense plastic foam from a packing box could also be used, but some of the loose-grained plastics tend to fall apart easily.

To keep the fly box from flopping around or blowing away, I keep it under the piece of bungee cord that secures my chart and tide table plastic envelopes (see page 22).

OTHER LURE-KEEPING AND STORAGE IDEAS

• A clear partitioned plastic box with a lid can be placed near the angler for the "hot" lures of the moment.   Pieces of rubber conveyor belt glued to the bottom of the box keep it from skidding.

• Small compartments in the top of Plano® Guide Series tackle boxes have a clear partitioned box built into the top of the larger tackle box.

• Bass anglers often clamp a piece of pipe insulating foam around the pedestal of their seats or leaning posts to hold favored lures.

• Clay Gooch of St. Michaels, MD clamped pipe insulation around the center pipe braces under his T-top to hold lures.

• A small compartmental plastic box can be rigged as a "belly box" with a belt for wade fishing. Commercial models are avail- able in fly-fishing catalogs.

• Steel shelves in the garage are winter storage for #3700 Plano boxes and other plastic boxes of boat gear.

• Heavy-duty zipper-lock plastic bags in a variety of sizes keep lure hooks from snagging.

• Department stores sell a variety of plastic containers in all sizes to fit your storage needs:

♦ Laundry baskets store anchors rigged with chain and rope.

♦ Small watertight boxes can be used for first aid materials.

♦ Use plastic shoe boxes to store large offshore lures.

♦ Larger storage containers hold rolled or folded plastic side curtains or life preservers.

♦ Golf club tubes or PVC pipe store rolled charts.

READY-RIGGED FLY RODS ON A BOAT

Most under-gunwale rod holders won't accommodate ready-rigged nine- or 10-foot long fly rods. While storing a separated two-piece fly rod is easy, it can be difficult to rig when fish are breaking all around the boat.

On my 22-foot walkaround cuddy, I use hook and loop wraps to secure a nine-foot fly rod to the bow rail stanchions. These wraps can be purchased in boat stores, or made at home with scraps of boat canvas and pieces of hook and loop fastener.

My wife made several wraparound strip fasteners, about 10" long and 1-1/2" wide, of doubled and sewn Sunbrella® boat canvas. She then sewed a 2" patch of "hook" on the inside at one end, and a 2" patch of "loop" on the other end on the outside. Length and width can be adjusted as needed.

In use, I tuck the fly rod inside the bow rail, then wrap one fastener around an upright and the fly rod near the reel seat and another near the rod tip and an upright near the bow. This system has held my fly rod securely in some really rough water. When I spot breaking fish, I simply pull off the fasteners and my rigged fly rod is ready for action!

TIPS FOR FLY FISHING ABOARD BOATS

"Use a large plastic laundry basket on a boat's deck as a stripping basket," says C. Boyd Pfeiffer. "Put about an inch of water in the bottom of the basket to stabilize the fly line; the extra weight will also keep the basket from sliding around."

• Cleats on boats attract fly lines. Captain Norm Bartlett of Baltimore, MD tapes a rubber snubber, minus the hooks, to a cleat and lets it dangle over the cleat ends.

• Fly fishers often snag their fly lines and leaders on various boat projections like cleats, cooler handles, or rod holders. Lefty Kreh carries a roll of masking tape with him to cover these snags temporarily. Lefty also occasionally uses a piece of netting as a cover. Boyd Pfeiffer made removable covers out of pieces of packing foam hollowed out to fit over cleats, etc. D. L. Goddard uses a large, wet beach towel over snags for the same reason.

• Cover the outside rails of a boat's T-top with foam pipe insulation to protect fly rod tips.

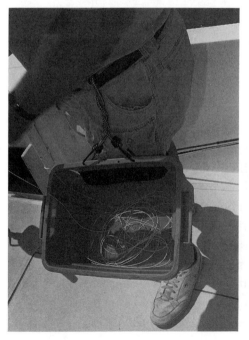

• Fly shop owner Joe Bruce of Baltimore, MD made the stripping basket on the left from a medium-sized laundry basket, attached to his side low-down (like a gunslinger's holster) by bungee cord ties.

• I made a stripping basket from an old plastic dishpan by cutting slots in its side. A 1" wide nylon web belt was threaded through the slots to go around my waist.

• A piece of outdoor carpet laid on the boat's deck will keep stripped fly line from tangling. Be sure and keep feet off the line!

VERSATILE LIVE BAITWELL

Most anglers have an occasional need to keep baitfish alive, but all of us don't have the space to make a permanent livewell installation in our boats. My solution to the problem is an easily removable, inexpensive live baitwell system that takes little space in the boat, and stores ashore when not needed.

Most sea water circulating systems have three basic parts:

1. A livewell. I use two: A 32-gallon plastic trash can and lid serves for large baits like live bluefish for king mackerel, and a smaller 20-gallon screw-top plastic jug that is ideal for minnows and silversides.

2. A pump to move the water: Mine is a small 400 gallon per hour (GPH) bilge pump attached to the lower leg of my outboard motor above the cavitation plate.

3. Piping to connect the pump to the livewell and provide a drain overboard: Input lines are made of 3/4" PVC pipe and fittings attached to an old 3/4" garden hose with couplings. The overboard drain is an old automobile radiator hose.

LIVEWELL: First, I determined the locations for the holes in each livewell by placing it in a suitable location in the boat. I drilled two holes with a hole saw in the side of the trash can (and the jug, too) about four inches below the lip. A 1-3/4" hole fits the 1-1/4" ABS pipe-to-male-thread adaptor which inserts into the auto radiator hose overboard drain, and one 1-1/8" hole to fit the 3/4" PVC input water pipe.

A short piece of 3/4" PVC input water pipe extends through the smaller hole in the side of the livewell. This connection was left uncemented so I could remove it later. Outside the hole, a PVC pipe-to-male-thread fitting connects to a female garden hose repair coupling. A suitable length of 3/4" hose connects to the bilge pump. Once the garden hose couplings are installed a short length of garden hose can be used to extend the distance between the bilge pump and the livewell.

Inside the livewell, a 90-degree 3/4" PVC ell and an 18" pipe extension angles downward to provide fresh sea water to the bottom of the livewell. Then, the water flows upward to drain overboard from the top. This removes fish gurry and scales. Very little water sloshes out if the can's lid is secured with a piece of shock cord. An aquarium-sized dip net or a trout net will reach the baitfish easily.

PUMP: An L-shaped stainless steel plate has appropriate holes drilled to attach the small bilge pump to the lower leg of the outboard motor above the cavitation plate. Electric 12 volt wiring was extended by soldering longer wires to the bilge pump wiring, and heatshrink tubing covers the connection. A polarized male plug was attached to the longer wires, and a mating female receptacle was installed on the bulkhead above the boat's battery compartment. Be sure to maintain correct wiring polarity—on my pump the brown wire with an inline fuse holder goes to the positive battery terminal and the white wire is connected to the negative side.

EXTERIOR PIPING: One obvious problem is the pump is out of the water when the boat is on plane. To solve that problem some anglers attach a piece of 1/2" copper pipe to the transom so that the open end of a 90-degree ell will face into the slipstream rushing from under the boat. A "Y" valve supplies water from the copper pipe when the boat is on plane, or from the pump when slow-trolling or at anchor.

Another option is to substitute a "T" for the manually-operated "Y" valve and include a one-way valve to prevent water from draining back overboard through the underway pickup when the boat is at rest.

The 20-gallon jug I use on the newer 22-foot boat is basically the same as far as plumbing and wiring are concerned. I clamped a piece of 1/4" galvanized hardware cloth over the drain to keep minnows from escaping. I also drilled a 1/16" hole near the top of the PVC water supply pipe just inside the jug so the water wouldn't siphon back overboard.

Running a small bilge pump all day on the engine-starting battery can run it down. A separate battery for the pump or a dual battery hookup provides an extra measure of safety.

My live baitwell system is easily removed and stored when it is not needed. All of the parts store in an onion sack and the trash can is used as such. The 32-gallon can will keep bluefish baits active and vigorous all day, and the smaller 20-gallon jug keeps even very fragile baits like silversides alive and frisky.

32-Gallon Livewell

←——————

20-Gallon Livewell

——————→

GAFF KEEPER

Shock cord is used for many things on our boats, but I found that one of the best uses for it is to keep a six-foot gaff handy and safely stored.

After placing a gaff in several locations in my 20-foot center console Mako, I decided that one of the handiest places was just above the under-gunwhale rod storage. Next I considered several ways of keeping it in place when the boat is under way in rough water. Stainless steel spring clips or brackets would protrude too far into the narrow aisle alongside the console and their sharp metal edges could threaten trousers or legs.

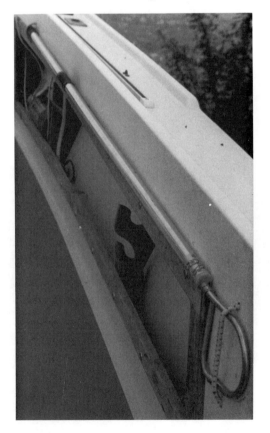

My solution was to drill two holes through the boat's inner sidewalls for the shock cord that would support each end of the gaff, or a total of four holes, slightly larger than the diameter of the shock cord. Before drilling, I made sure that I could get to the back of the sidewalls to tie knots in the shock cord. A suitable length of shock cord was knotted on one end and the unknotted end was passed through one of the holes from the back side, then threaded through the other hole. After pulling that end tight from the back to provide suitable tension, I tied a knot in it. This was done for each end of the gaff. The gaff is stored under the loops in the shock cord, safely out of the way.

⚠ A stainless steel spring wire coil, attached to the gaff hook, covers the needle-sharp hook point until the gaff is needed.

• • • • • • • • • • • • • • • • •

SEATBACK SAFETY HANDLES

Adding grab handles to the backs of the seats on my center console Mako solved a potential safety problem for me. There is nothing for a passenger standing in the back of my boat to grab if the person driving hits the throttle suddenly. I found this out the hard way; by the next weekend I had safety handles installed.

My safety grab handles were made of stainless steel 3/4" i. d. stainless steel pipe, bent into a "U" shape for me by a friend with a conduit bender. To fit my boat seats, each handle is 11" wide and 14" high, outside dimensions. Your dimensions may be different.

The U-shaped handles were mounted on the backs of the seats with the open side of the "U" facing downward. I allowed 2" of clearance between the top of the seat and the top of the handle. To allow 1" of clearance from the seatback, I made 4 standoffs 1" long for each seat handle from the same stainless steel pipe, for a total of 8 stand-offs. One end of each stand-off was scalloped so that it would fit against the curved pipe of the handle.

Mounted to the back of a standard boat seat, a
U-shaped handle provides a handy safety bar.

Holes to accommodate the 1/4"-20 by 3 in. long stainless
steel cap screws were drilled 1" and 6" from the bottom of the
inverted "U" handle. After positioning the handles properly on
the seat back, bolt holes were drilled through the seat. Cap
screws were inserted from the seat side and the seatback cushion
covered the screw heads for comfort. Then, I cut the cap screws
to length and used rounded cap nuts on the handle side for a
nicer appearance. For additional safety, I put a dab of epoxy in
each nut before assembly.

ROD HOLDERS

Rod holders on boats keep the long wands out of the way, yet handy to the angler. Those who grab up a bundle of rods and dump them in a tangled pile on the boat will live to regret it, most notably when fish are breaking water all around the boat and rods, lines, and lures are permanently entwined.

Most mid-sized fishing boats today have rod pockets under the gunwales. My 22-foot walk-around cuddy cabin hull has no under-gunwale rod pockets. The longer I have the hull, the more I like the plain bulkheads in the fishing area. Like most anglers in a hurry, I once simply tossed a bundle of rods in the starboard side walkway around the cabin. It seemed like a logical place—the VHF-FM radio antenna is on that side and no one walks around that side, anyway. So, I installed a six-rod holder on that side where there had always been a tangle of rods.

Next, in the cabin, I installed two sets of teak 4-rod holders on the bulkheads beside the bunks with short stainless steel square-drive screws, plus epoxy. Mounting gunwale rod holders was quite a challenge, but I think just about anyone handy with tools can do the job. I first determined the best locations for gunwale-top rod holders. Then, I lightly pencilled four positions for the holders, two on each side on the gunwale tops. I checked my measurements from the transom so the holes were evenly placed. The aft two holders faced the stern, and the front ones were angled outboard slightly so their rod's lures would track outside the rear rods.

Luckily, the new rod holders came in an angled plastic package that also served as an excellent drill guide (see top photo on page 46). A 1/4" hole was drilled in the center of the bottom of the holder package, and an 18" long, 1/4-inch diameter drill bit was aligned through the center of the clear plastic package, which when placed against the gunwale top, luckily gave the same, correct angle for the rod holders. Pilot holes were drilled in the gunwale top for a hole saw's guide bit. ⚠ Do not use a hole saw without this centering bit—it can whip around out of the hole and hurt you!

Drilling the pilot holes for the flush-mounted gunwale rod holders.

Drilling the holes in the gunwale top for a rod holder.

With the hole saw's guide bit aligned in the pilot hole, a 1-3/4" hole was drilled in the gunwale top for each rod holder. I used an electric drill for this job, since the hole saw required so much power (see lower photo on page 46).

⚠ The boat was on the trailer—never use a 110 volt power tool aboard with the boat in the water! In that case, use only battery-powered or air-powered tools.

My hull was packed with foam flotation all the way up under the gunwale, so it required a lot of digging to get enough space for the rod holders. Next, I fit the rod holders in place and drilled pilot holes for three mounting screws for each holder. To keep water from running into the foam inside the gunwale, I taped the bottom end of each rod holder, set it up vertically, and carefully poured in a thin coat of epoxy to seal the bottom.

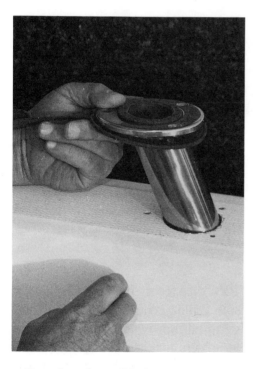

Securing the rod holders in place.

When the epoxy set up, the rod holders were screwed down in place, and their rubber covering flaps secured over the rod sockets.

Next, the flat plates for two stainless steel demountable holders were secured, one on each side, to the cabin's exterior bulkheads. The holders are stored in the cabin unless needed for two rods sticking out to the sides when trolling.

Two more bulkhead-mount tube holders were screwed to the aft bulkhead, and a recessed rod holder was mounted on the after surface of each side of the cabin bulkhead, both facing aft. These are handy when the seats are rotated to face the stern for drift-fishing. The hull came with only two rod holders—surface mounted tubes installed on an aft bulkhead. Now, I can store 26 rods in holders, although I only use about 18 different rods on a given fishing day!

All of those already installed on the boat were commercial rod holders, but someone handy with PVC pipe or teak can make rod holders for about any placement ashore or aboard. For instance, I made PVC rod holders for a fishing bench at the end of my dock, and I've seen teak rod holders mounted in beach-buggy ceilings that rival the nicest factory-mades.

Jim Price has rod holders of PVC pipe recessed into the front deck of his 20-foot Mako center console fishing boat shown above. They keep rods out of the way of his Bimini top, which is always up.

Other anglers make PVC rod holders for their boats, and mount them in places that are out of the way, yet accessible. Some beach anglers have adapted PVC pipe for rod hangers on the "bow" of their favorite sand vehicle, but surf angler "Peanut" Sullivan of Berlin, Maryland mounted rod holders angling aft on each side of the rear fenders on his Chevy Blazer beach buggy.

Surf anglers often use 3- or 4-foot pieces of 1-1/2" diameter PVC pipe for sand spikes. They cut one end on a 30- or 45-degree angle so it will penetrate beach sand, and cut a slot for a reel foot in the opposite end. Shorter versions are used as rod holders on the front of beach buggies so ready-rigged outfits are handy to the action. Sand the burr off the inside top rim of the pipe until it's smooth so it doesn't abrade your rod handles.

Home-brew PVC pipe rod holders should have two mounting holes to stabilize the holder and keep it from turning sideways under stress. Drill a small hole in one side of the pipe to accommodate the screw size you will use, then drill a larger hole opposite that one large enough to accommodate a screwdriver. Repeat those holes far enough apart to assure stability when mounted. For mounting, I use tapered-head square-drive stainless screws recessed

Captain Mike Murphy displays a nice trout caught on a rod stored in one of the many rod holders installed on his boat.

flush so rod handles aren't damaged when bounced around in a seaway. A lengthways slot can be cut for an inch or two from the top of the holder to engage a spinning or levelwind reel foot and keep it from spinning around in the holder.

I have also used 1-5/8" inside diameter thin wall plastic pipe made for home central vacuum systems for rod holders. It is easy to work with, but it won't take as much abuse as Schedule 40 PVC water pipe. Thin wall tube can be flared at one end by heating it in boiling water, or if careful with a heat gun, and rotating it around a heavyweight tin funnel to force a flared end in the tubing. This tubing can also be used for light duty sand spikes or rod holders in a jon boat.

• • • • • • • • • • • • • • •

UPDATE: COKING CAN ZAP YOUR OUTBOARD!

New low-octane and alcohol-blend fuels are trashing the insides of your outboard motor every time you run it, according to recent news releases by major engine manufacturers and BOAT/U.S. But there is help—it's called preventive maintenance. Read on.

When lead was removed from gasoline, it may have helped the environment, but it was bad news for marine engines, particularly outboards.

The late Jerry Lewis was Service Manager at Fred Quimby Marine Sales in Easton, Maryland in 1992. He showed several outboard motor pistons to a local fishing club. The first piston's rings were stuck. The second showed scoring on the piston skirt. The third (shown in the photo on the opposite page) was in an outboard destroyed by low quality fuel .

Lewis said all of the pistons came from the same engine, a 200 hp Yamaha, but he was quick to point out that all engine manufacturers were having the same problem. "It is not an engine problem," Jerry said, "It is a fuel problem." High horsepower two-cycle outboards mix oil and gasoline in the combustion chamber, and high compression levels combine with the extra heat generated

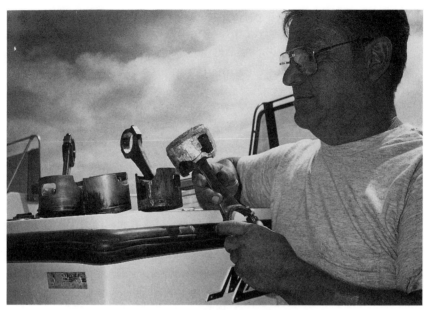

Jerry Lewis with destroyed piston.

by two-cycle engines builds up carbon. That carbon sticks the rings. Engineers call it *"coking."* When the rings seize, blowby and piston slap score cylinder walls and piston skirts. Next, something cuts loose inside the engine, causing the last mutilated piston Lewis showed us. That engine required a new power head—an expensive job. Those repairs were covered by the manufacturer under warranty.

Problems arise for those of us who own older engines no longer covered under warranty. Is your outboard several years old? Has it been fed 87-octane gas? If so, it is probably time for a compression check of each cylinder by your friendly mechanic.

If it is running unevenly, or lacks the power it once had, don't walk to your dealer—run! Don't let a blown motor ruin your day— or your summer.

The first thing your mechanic will do to an older motor, says Claude von Plato of Yamaha Marine, is to spray combustion chamber cleaner into the motor while it is running with water cooling it.

Then, the motor is shut down for a period of time to let the powerful cleaner work. When the engine is restarted, carbon deposits leave the motor with the cooling water. Do-it-yourself boaters should follow directions on the can.

"You can't do this every 100 hours and save the motor," von Plato said, "the chamber cleaning compound is a powerful solvent that attacks seals and gaskets." It is not nearly as good as a continuing treatment like [Yamaha] Ring Free® which is mixed 1 ounce to 8 gallons of gasoline and flushes carbon away as it cleans everything downstream, including the carburetor."

Yamaha, Mercury, and Outboard Marine Corporation (OMC, makers of Johnson and Evinrude motors) were painfully aware of the carbon problem. They found Chevron's Techroline® solvent would clean carbon deposits, and that product is now sold as Yamaha's Ring Free®, OMC's Carbon Guard®, and Mercury's Quicksilver Power Tune®.

A 12-ounce bottle of those products (essentially the same, though von Plato says Ring Free® is more concentrated) will treat about 96 gallons of gasoline, but be sure and read the label for individual instructions.

New OMC motors, according to Chuck Merritt of OMC Public Relations, should be started with Carbon Guard® in the gas "from day one."

Mechanically-minded boaters asked why these solvents couldn't just be included in the TC-W2® rated outboard oil everyone used in the early 1990s, so we boaters wouldn't forget the important additive.

OMC, Yamaha, and Mercury cooperated on a solvent/lube oil blend that was labelled TC-W3® in 1992. Problems arose when they were not able to include enough solvent in the oil without changing its lubricating properties, so Ring Free® and the other solvents still must be added to your gas.

OMC recommends using Carbon Guard® in both two- and four-cycle engines, according to Michael M. Potter of OMC Management. But, if an owner has more than 100 hours on his engine before using Carbon Guard®, OMC recommends first treating the engine with their Engine Tuner®. Then, add Carbon Guard® to the gas on subsequent fill-ups.

Mike Walker, who handles Public Relations for Yamaha, says he uses Ring Free® in his Chevy Suburban towing vehicle. "Put the recommended amount in your tank with a fill-up," Walker says, "then run the tank until it's almost empty. It makes a big difference in performance. But, when that tank of gas is gone, von Plato said it's a good idea to change the oil." I wonder if my 1989 Chevy, its wheezy old V-8 engine clocking 120,000 miles, would tolerate that much cleaning. Carbon might be the only thing holding it together. And, it would be wise to check with your auto dealer before doing that much cleaning in an electronic fuel injection (EFI) system. However, premium gas (93 octane) is said to include cleaners.

Engine manufacturers, according to BOAT/U.S., will not guarantee engines if they are run on "low quality fuels," but how can Joe Angler detect a "low quality fuel?" Would you rather take a chance? What to do?

Tell you what I will do with my new 1998, 175 hp Johnson FICHT outboard motor. I will mix Carbon Guard® with my gasoline, use OMC's TC-W3® rated oil, and use the recommended OMC Engine Tuner® every 50 hours or so. No way can I afford to replace an outboard engine that cost more than our first house did in 1958!

NOTE: This article was first published in 1992 and this updated version published in 1998. Because technology is changing daily, outboard motor owners should contact their dealers for current recommendations about solvents to use or not use with their gasoline.

HONEYCOMB PLUG HOLDER

There is no joy in having a lively fish attached to the tail hook of your treble hook plug when the other hook is embedded in your finger. To avoid this painful embarrassment, I devised a system that keeps me at a safe distance from treble hooks and sharp-toothed fish.

My system begins with a spinning or baitcasting outfit and some treble hook plugs. I re-arm my plugs with sharp stainless steel treble hooks—or a single tail hook for catch and release fishing. For toothy fish, I tie about 24" of braided wire leader directly to the lure with a figure-eight knot, or crimp a loop with leader sleeves. At the end of the wire leader I make another loop that snaps to the end of my fishing line.

For toothless fish to be coolered, a heavy mono leader could be used. If we have found and hooked up with big, toothy bluefish, we leader the fish into the cooler and slam the lid with the wire leader sticking out. Then, we can safely unsnap the snap swivel at the end of the running line and snap on another plug and get back in business. Lures are retrieved when the fish calms down. To keep the plugs from tangling in this melee, I made a honeycomb plug holder from 1-5/8 inch i.d. PVC electrical conduit with 1/2-inch sheet PVC for the bottom and back. My holder has been mounted on two boats, in back of the seat on my 16-foot Whaler, and inside the anchor locker door on my 20-foot Mako.

To make the plug holder, I cut 21 pieces of the PVC conduit into eight-inch lengths and arranged the pieces in staggered rows, like a honeycomb, for strength. The bottom and the mounting straps in the back were cut from the sheet PVC. All parts were assembled and glued with standard PVC cement. Small holes were drilled in the bottom of the tubes for drainage.

When I transferred the holder from the Whaler to the Mako, I simply cut off two of the end conduits so the holder would fit the anchor locker door.

A plug holder like mine could be assembled from many other materials: Schedule 40 PVC water pipe, plexiglas, copper, or even stainless steel.

Plug holder mounted on the back of the Boston Whaler seat.

Plug holder mounted on the back of the Mako anchor locker door.

CONSOLE TOP ORGANIZER

A compartmental Plexiglas® tray about 2" deep, 6" wide, and 13" long helps organize all the miscellaneous "small stuff" that use to rattle around on (and eventually fall off) the top of the center console on my fishing boat. A few small squares of double-sided foam tape of the type artists use to mount pictures can be used to hold the tray down in rough seas, but are easy to remove.

The many small sections in the tray accommodate the variety of tiny items one usually has to dig for in a tackle box or pockets. The tray was originally labelled as a cosmetics organizer, but a similar tray could be built for your boat. Almost any material the tackle tinkerer has at hand would do the job. Even a kitchen drawer insert used to organize knives and forks will work. The only change I made was to drill a small hole in the bottom of each section for drainage.

If you need some special design for a hard-to-fit place, you can make your own organizer from 1/4" thick Plexiglas® sheet. Check with a plastics shop for the proper sawing technique and the proper solvent for your material.

A recent inventory of the contents of my organizer revealed the following items: Six sizes of snaps and snap swivels, four different types of sinkers in assorted weights, several small spoons and bucktail jigs, two sharpening stones, a stainless steel multi-function knife, an extra boat drain plug, and a boat gas cap key. If a small item needs to be handy it's in my organizer!

• • • • • • • • • • • • •

SEVERAL ELECTRIC MOTOR INSTALLATIONS

Anglers drifting for flounder and other bottom-feeders know their bait must be moving across the bottom, and they must cover a lot of bottom unless the fish are really thick. But, when wind and tide are slack a minnow is allowed to sit still on the bottom too long—it gets a chance to look around and find something to hide under. Keep the bait moving, say the experts.

A small outboard motor will work, or you can use a small, quiet electric motor and avoid the noise and oil fumes from a two-cycle gas engine. Several years ago, I bought a transom-mount Minn Kota 35M electric for the 14-foot jon boat I use for bass fishing in protected waters. Later, I found the same motor also moves my 22-foot fiberglass hull on Chesapeake Bay at flounder-catching speed on days when we are becalmed by wind and current.

Small electric motors usually have alligator clips on the power leads, and some anglers carry a spare deep-cycle battery to use with their small motor. I substituted a polarized heavy duty plug for the clips, then mounted a compatible receptacle just above the two-battery compartment near the transom on my 22 foot boat. I caution you to use wire heavy enough to handle your electric motor's considerable current draw for the leads between the battery and receptacle, and use a proper fuse. Undersize wire can cause a fire when overheated. Byrd Industries calculated that the thrust on a

12-volt motor, with about 18 feet of battery cable, will increase about 34 percent when the heavier 4-gauge wire is substituted for 12-gauge. Byrd also suggests keeping the battery cable as short as possible.

By using 4-gauge wire instead of 12-gauge, you could improve performance beyond 40 percent. Also, determine whether your electric motor needs 12, 24, or 36 volts, then follow the motor's installation directions and wiring diagrams accordingly. To use the small electric motor on my small jon boat, I have a spare battery with a compatible polarized receptacle mounted on the top of its plastic case.

Technically-inclined anglers will notice in the photograph of my 22 foot boat's stern that I rotated the electric motor's shaft 180 degrees. I can reach the aft-facing handle in my small jon boat from the bow seat; and it's no problem to reach the handle facing aft on the big boat's transom.

My small electric motor was not designed for heavy duty in saltwater. Even so, it has held up well for eight summers. Recently I bought a Minn Kota RT36/S electric motor with a stainless steel shaft and other parts; it promises long service in the salt. It has a KotaStow bracket that allows me to raise the motor halfway—enough to have it out of the water when the boat is on plane as we run back for another drift. Even so, I always attach a safety rope to the electric in case the transom screws work loose.

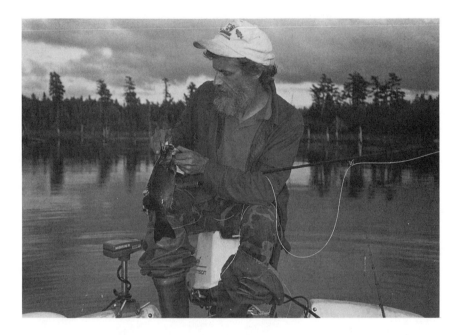

Guide Perry Munro (above) of Wolfville, Nova Scotia, mounts his electric motor on the transom of his 14-foot Whaler. This gives his anglers in the bow first shot at the water. Bow-mounted electrics give the *guide* first shot.

MAKING A NEW PEDESTAL SEAT BASE

When the bolts loosened that held the pedestal seats on my 1974 20-foot Mako, I was afraid a seat might pull loose on acceleration and injure someone. The wood backer plate for the seat screws under the fiberglass deck had rotted due to water intrusion, but the wood was between two molded-in bait tanks in the after deck and an underdeck gas tank forward and therefore inaccessible. To get to the rotten wood I would have had to remove the console and the cover plate under it, then remove the gas tank—a considerable job.

Instead, with considerable help from Jack Stovall, we made a new base from two pieces of 5/4" teak, glued edge-to-edge to make a piece that was wide enough and long enough to accommodate the two pedestal seats. Then, the top and corners of the teak board were rounded with a router. Next, fifty 3/4" diameter holes were drilled about 1/2" deep with a sharp Forstner bit to accommodate fifty 3/4" diameter plugs made from a piece of scrap teak. Smaller

holes were drilled through the center of the bottom of the 3/4"
holes for stainless steel screws that would anchor the seat base to,
and through, the fiberglass deck.

A pencil line was drawn around the completed seat base on the
boat deck so it would be easy to quickly put the base in place when
epoxy was applied to the deck and the bottom surface of the base.

West System® two-part clear epoxy was applied to the deck and
bottom of the base, the base lined up with the pencilled lines, and
50 screws pulled the base down tight. Once the epoxy set up, the
screw-covering plugs were painted with epoxy and tapped in to
cover the screw heads, leaving 1/8" or so of each wood plug sticking
up above the teak base. Once the epoxy applied to the plugs set up,
the plugs were sanded off flush for a neat job.

Next, the seat bases were lag-screwed into the new teak base,
and the seat pedestals secured to the bases.

The installation was sturdy and secure. The seats had no play
in them, even with a 200-pound man trying to rock them back and
forth. One additional advantage was the extra 1-1/4" of seat height
gave the captain better visibility over the console windshield.

MARINE RADIO INSTALLATIONS

A gradual shift from Citizen's Band (CB) radios to very high frequency (VHF) sets has helped us pass on fishing hot spots to our buddies.   There were so many CB sets in autos and trucks that airwaves became too crowded for reliable communications, so mariners left CB for VHF.

During the transition from CB to VHF, I installed one of each type radio in the glove compartment of my 20-foot Mako. I cut away part of the back wall of the glove compartment for wiring, and removed the entire unit for winter storage. One radio had its speaker in the bottom of the set, so it was mounted on the top of the compartment. Since the other radio's speaker was in the top of the set, it was mounted on the bottom of the compartment, so each one would broadcast toward the center of the compartment. (The glove compartment shows in the lower right-hand corner of the "Console Top Organizer" idea on page 56).

My present VHF radio is installed through the bulkhead near the steering wheel on my 22-foot walkaround cuddy hull. It has a water-resistant front panel and all the controls are on the front of the set. Woe is me if I have a problem with the set since it is weatherproofed (read permanently caulked in) with 3M 5200 Marine Adhesive Sealant®.

My criteria for a VHF radio for the boat included a front panel speaker (a large remote extension speaker gives better reception), a numeric keypad so I could immediately change channels, and a front panel microphone plug. Since most of the anglers in our area have switched to VHF, the local good 'ol boys have returned to CB radios for a modicum of security. The really good stuff is relayed via cell phone!

The small triangular bulkhead just inside the cabin door on the right side in the 22-foot Angler was just large enough to mount a marine version of an AM/FM cassette-tape radio. Luckily, the boat's wiring center is just behind that bulkhead. Speakers for this radio are flush mounted on the bulkheads on either side of the steering station.

LOCKER COVER REPAIRS

Boat manufacturers often use plywood or end-grain balsa wood as stiffeners under locker or baitwell covers, especially those that can be walked on.

My 1974 Mako hull had two bait tanks built under the deck behind the seats. Their removeable covers were reinforced with small pieces of balsa wood, encapsulated with another layer of fiberglass on the underside. After the hull was about 15 years old the covers had taken quite a beating from constant walking, running— even jumping. The fiberglass developed cracks on the underside of the covers. This allowed moisture to seep into the balsa wood, which became mushy and ruined as a stiffener. I took out all of the balsa and replaced it with 1/2" marine plywood, which was painted with several coats of West System® epoxy, then it was laminated together with the top and bottom layers of fiberglass as it had been originally.

The same thing has happened to my latest hull, the 22-foot Horizon by Angler. Two lockers with hinged covers are handy places to store things or can even be made into baitwells. But, they are located in high traffic areas of the boat and are also a handy place to jump on when getting aboard.

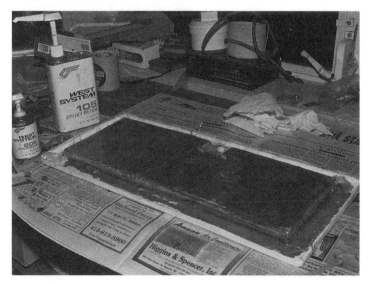

The covers were stiffened with plywood, but the constant pounding from 200-pounds-plus anglers soon cracked the fiberglass encapsulation around the 3/8" plywood. In this case, the fix was simpler. The 3/8" plywood was replaced with stronger 3/4" plywood. West System® epoxy was painted on the plywood (two coats) and the new plywood was covered with fiberglass cloth. It was wetted with two coats of epoxy. After curing, the encapsulated wood was painted with exterior white latex. White gel coat would have been another overcoat option. See photo on page 63.

Many other cracks or fissures on boats can be repaired in similar fashion. If in doubt about how to proceed, contact your local boating supply store for directions and materials.

•••••••••••••

CAN AND CUP HOLDERS

Spilled beverages in the boat can make a sticky mess, sometimes bad enough to draw flies.

Holders can be quickly made in the home shop to accommodate beverages in can coolers, mugs, or "sippers."

PVC Schedule 40 pipe of the proper inside diameter (i. d.) is one option, though a bit heavy. Another possibility is 4-inch i. d. thin wall sewer pipe. I made a simple holder from a 4-1/2 inch length of new sewer drainfield pipe and an end cap and attached it to the top of the console on my 22-foot walkaround cuddy cabin hull with double-sided foam mounting tape. It is large enough to hold any mug or can cooler I use. It holds beverages in place in rough seas, though any container with an open top is bound to slosh out some liquid in a sloppy seaway.

Cup holders can also be made from sheet polyethylene or woods like teak or mahogany which survive in the marine environment. An ingenious bulkhead-mount cup holder I saw in a catalog was made of three pieces of wood, and folds up when not in use.

ONE ANGLER'S MARINE ELECTRONICS

My friend Marty Jester stared at me in disbelief when I explained how I had wired the electronics on the 16-foot Boston Whaler I had 34 years ago.

"I had a CB radio, a flasher depthfinder, and navigation lights," I told Marty. "I ran two lengths of 4-gauge cable from the engine through the Whaler's tunnel to the battery that was wedged under the front seat." So far, so good. "Then, I took some brown lamp cord (Marty stopped his sandwich halfway to his mouth) and ran it from the battery to the switches on the console (he began to choke), and hooked up the radio and depthfinder with those little blue things (choke, choke) you squeeze together to connect wires."

I had the feeling that he disapproved. Marty, who has installed marine electronics and electrical equipment since 1973 on every kind of watercraft from Exxon tankers to fishing boats, and now owns Mid-Shore Electronics in Cambridge, MD, was frowning. "Was that a no-no?" I asked. "A big no-no," he replied.

Lamp cord is not an approved wire for marine use. Marty recommends marine grade tinned wire. "You should also use the right crimping tool and connectors," he said. "And, wire connections exposed to the weather or bilges should be covered with heatshrink tubing that has a sealer incorporated."

While I got away with my shade-tree mechanic's marginal practices for several years, I did have a lot of potentially troublesome electronic equipment failures on my older boats that were caused by corroded connections.

I asked Marty about the most common electrical problems he is called upon to fix. "Boat manufacturers often use a minimum size of wire to keep their prices down," Marty said. "Undersized wiring is one of the biggest problems we've had over the years. When you start adding accessories like washdown pumps, radios, spotlights, and other goodies, the wiring often won't carry the load. You don't get proper performance and you've shortened the life span of your equipment."

I explained that on my previous 20-foot Mako hull I gathered up all the loose wires under the console and tied them to the steering cable to get them out of the way.

"That does provide some strain relief," Marty said, "wiring shouldn't hang by its connectors." The problem reappears when a new steering cable is installed and the wires are cut loose, and not reattached.

On my Mako, I noticed the compass was affected by the nearby VHF radio's speaker magnet on a trial placement. I had to move the radio to the opposite side of the console to avoid magnetic interference.

Marty just installed a complete electronics package on a 36-foot Stamas and offered to show it to me when we finished lunch. What planning must be done before cutting a lot of holes in a new boat's command center?

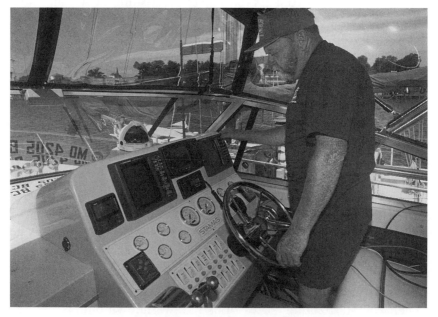

Marty Jester at the console of a 36-foot Stamus.

"We work with owners to decide what their final goals are," Marty said. "We leave room for future installations, make sure everything is within reach of the helm, that nothing obstructs the operator's view. We make doubly sure there is room behind the panel for surface mounted units."

What about the average guy who wants to install his own electronics? I installed the electronics on all my boats, first the 16-foot Whaler, then a 20-foot Mako, and lately on my 22-foot walkaround cuddy hull. As I upgraded boats, I also added more gear and equipment.

My 1964 Whaler had Marty's minimum recommended electronic package for anglers—lighting package, compass, depthfinder, and a (CB) radio. The compass and depthfinder, I learned in the Power Squadron's Basic and Advanced Piloting courses, can be used in combination with charts to estimate your approximate location. The radio is backup in case all else fails.

Our 1974 Mako had a compass, depthfinder, two radios (CB and VHF),Loran, one bilge pump, two batteries with a switch, plus lots of neat switches and gauges. Wiring was a bit messy, but I knew where it all was and it never let me down. The loose wires were gathered together and secured to the steering cable. The boat served me well for 18 years.

To keep various antennas to a minimum so I could cast lures 360 degrees around the boat, I substituted a 40-inch piece of 1/4-inch diameter stainless steel rod for the Loran-C antenna that usually screws into the end of the bottle-shaped preamp at the end of the long cable. I read in *Salt Water Sportsman* magazine that someone used his bow rail as a substitute Loran antenna, so I tried that. Didn't work for me. The 40-inch long rod worked. I hid it under the gunwale above the Mako's rod pocket. Later, I installed my makeshift antenna horizontally in the 22-foot Angler cabin. These installations are not factory recommended. One should use an antenna matched to the electronic instrument. But, the combination worked for me for 16 years.

Our recent 22-foot Angler hull has the same compliment of electronics, less a CB radio, but I added a cell phone and an AM/FM radio with a tape deck. Wiring is neatly connected to a wiring bus behind the instrument panel and tied together to provide strain relief. Any wiring connections I made have been soldered and covered with shrink tubing, which adds to my confidence, but would run up labor costs on a yard installation. The new Johnson 175 FICHT engine takes a lot of juice so I use two MCA-1000 rated batteries. The battery switch is set on "both" when the boat is in use. With the previous smaller batteries, starting the engine took power away from the depthfinder, cell phone, and Loran, so they had to restart themselves with a "beep" or two.

My Loran has become somewhat forgetful. When it said I was at waypoint 11 (our dock), I was still 5 miles down the creek. This is not a great way to find your way home in the fog. I later found that the antenna plug was corroded and needed a little "TLC" in the form of cleaning, plus some resoldering inside the unit, to give me back the excellent signal-to-noise ratio (SNR) I had when the unit was new.

"Get a GPS," Marty said. "I don't know of a single manufacturer who is still making Loran units—and GPS prices are coming down every day." Global Position System (GPS), as most people know, has a built-in "dithering," or inaccuracy, of 100 meters (over 300 feet), so our enemies can't use the space satellite-based system against us. Seems to me that an atomic bomb landing 300 feet from a target could still do a fair amount of damage. An add-on unit called "DGPS" can accurize the GPS.

Recent discussions in *Boat/U.S. Magazine* about shutting down the Loran system indicate it would be more costly to shut it down in the year 2000 than to keep it operating until at least 2015. Boat/ U.S. also makes the case that there are so many Loran units in use that shutting the system down would cause a major safety hazard. All this can be changed, but I plan to run dual systems, Loran and GPS, until that day.

So, I bought a Lowrance GlobalMap 1600 GPS. It has a reasonably large screen (4 inches square) and maps of my home area are already installed. In addition, I can load other maps and even offshore wrecks into the unit from a CD ROM that fits my computer. The GlobalMap 1600 has a magnet on the back of its hockey-puck size antenna so it will adhere to the top of my car, and road maps can be loaded so we can tell where we are when traveling. An extra power cord for the car is the only accessory we'll need. The 1600 mounting bracket is affixed to the boat on a 1/4-inch stud with a stainless steel wing nut so the GPS mounting bracket can easily be moved to a car.

Lowrance X70A Depthfinder on the left with a new Lowrance GlobalMap 1600 on the boat console.

The long cable to the GPS antenna is wound on an old plastic 16mm film reel for easy portability and less mess on the boat's console.

Thirty-four years ago, I was as happy as a Lab puppy with my minimal electronic accessories. Today, I have the bare minimum of gear for the way I fish, and I consider everything necessary. That's progress.

QUICK TIPS FOR ANGLERS

• A yardstick can be applied to a cooler or the fishing boat in a handy place, but the sun will bleach out the ink over time. If you can find one, a yardstick printed on plastic sheeting with an adhesive backing is ideal. I bought two at a fishing show for $1 each and sliced them longways to remove the advertising. The one on top of my starboard gunwale has been there since 1992 and still hasn't faded.

• In addition to the ruler on the gunwhale, other measuring devices on the cooler are an L-shaped board with a yardstick attached (the fish's nose goes against the upright board for accuracy), a "Florida Lawstick" from *Florida Sportsman* Magazine, and a free folding fish and crab ruler from the Maryland DNR. The Igloo® cooler also has a ruler molded into its top.

• Sooner or later, you will find mold and/or oil residue in your boat's bilge. Boating supply stores sell environmentally safe cleaners to use in the bilge. Some allow a little water and dish detergent to slosh around in the bilge if it can be safely drained later. Don't even think about draining oil overboard!

• Use your flasher-type depthsounder to indicate hard or soft bottom. Generally, fish will be over hard bottom, and uneven or oystershell bottom is often the best. First, turn down the sensitivity until you get only one bottom indication, with no "doubling." (Doubling occurs when the sensitivity is too high, and when the known depth is 30 feet—doubling will give two readings, one at 30 and another at 60 feet. This does not work with the new automatic LCD finders). With a single reading at 30 feet and the sensitivity turned back to show one reading over soft bottom, you will get doubling when the boat moves over hard bottom. The bottom reading will be "jagged," composed of different-width lines, or "blips" when showing uneven or oystershells.

• Flats boats can be equipped with an upside-down U-shaped leaning post of stainless steel pipe socketed into the front deck to give the angler something to lean against when tired and something to grab when tossed around by a wake.

• On my Angler walk-around cuddy there's a stepdown which is often unnoticed by guests or yours truly. To call attention to this stepdown I made my own "safety stripe" tape by applying a strip of yellow waterproof tape the width of the step then adding squares of black waterproof electrician's tape on top of the yellow strip.

• Consider carrying an extra battery as a backup. I often bring along a spare and use it to power my electric trolling motor if I plan to use it a lot. I lift it on the dock to recharge it, using an auto battery charger plugged into a GFCI breaker-protected outlet.

• I also carry a 4-gauge copper wire jumper cable set in a plastic storage container with a lid for backup in the boat. It is long enough to reach from my two battery-compartment to the battery in the next boat if both of my batteries are down. It has happened.

• If your outboard motor's oil tank is out of sight, install a dash-mounted oil level gauge so you can keep an eye on it. And, keep an extra gallon of outboard oil aboard just in case.

• Carry a tool kit and include fuses for your motor and dash.

The author with the catch of the day in his parallel-docked Boston Whaler.

PARALLEL BOAT DOCKING

In narrow waterways like canals, docks perpendicular to the shoreline are not practical, so I attached a parallel dock to the wooden bulkhead like a shelf. Two stainless steel pipe brackets held my 16-foot Boston Whaler and later a 20-foot Mako secure. Since relatively deep water was available right up to the bulkhead, my parallel-docked boats were afloat even at low tides.

First, a heavy-duty "shelf" was attached parallel to the wooden bulkhead. The pilings were about eight feet apart, so a span of three pilings gave me three "shelf" braces at 8-foot intervals. Since the decking boards overhung each end brace two feet or so, I had about a 20-foot dock.

Dock supports were made from creosoted 4 x 6 in. timbers bolted together and to the pilings with 5/8" galvanized bolts, nuts, and washers.

Recently, treated lumber for docks and piers has replaced creosoted lumber which is an ecological no-no here on the Chesapeake Bay. Check local regulations in your area.

Once the three dock supports were bolted to the pilings with their top surfaces level, I nailed 3 x 12 in. dressed scrap lumber on top of the supports as decking.

I had two stainless steel pipe-support brackets fabricated, one to be bolted to each end of the dock to secure the Whaler at bow and stern. Each bracket was made of three 12" square pieces of 1/4" thick stainless steel plate. A crosspiece of 1/2" round stainless pipe stock was welded to a 6" piece of 1-1/4" i. d. pipe held between the upright plates so it would pivot. A 5/16" hole was drilled vertically through the pivoting pipe for a 1/4" bolt. Holes were drilled in each corner of the bottom plates of the brackets for 5/8" bolts to fasten them to the dock.

Both standoff pipes were of 1" i. d. stainless steel. The stern pipe was long enough to reach from the starboard stern lifting eye on the Whaler to 6" beyond the shoreside bracket when the boat

STAINLESS STEEL BRACKET

(not to scale)

sliding pipe
(length to suit)

Near dock
bolt position

Pivot Pin

Away from dock
bolt position

Eye bolt & Rope
spliced to snap
to secure boat

was pushed off 24" from the dock. The bow pipe reached from the shoreside bracket to the boat's bow cleat.

Holes were then drilled in the standoff pipes for near (12" from the dock) and far (24" from the dock) boat locations. The 1/4" bolt was simply slipped through the captive pipe in each bracket, and through the 1" standoff pipe at the location where the boat would be secured. Holes were drilled in the outboard end of each standoff for galvanized eye bolts. Large galvanized snaps were spliced to each eye bolt with 1/2" nylon rope.

When docked, the ends of each standoff pipe were snapped to the Whaler's bow and stern. Pipes were slipped through the dock brackets until the boat was 24" away from the dock. Then the 1/4" bolts were placed through the standoff and dock bracket to secure. To draw the boat close enough to the dock to get aboard, the 1/4" bolts were removed and the pipes slipped back to the second bolt holes and secured with the 1/4" bolts. The pivoting 1-1/4" i. d. pipe inside the steel bracket allowed the boat to rise and fall with the tide.

The 20-foot Mako parallel-docked.

When the 20-foot Mako replaced the Whaler, the pipe brackets had to be moved farther apart, making it necessary to mount the brackets on the wooden bulkhead. The bow snap was also modified to fit the Mako. Docking or un-docking was a snap—or two.

BOAT SLIP DE-ICER

Several de-icers are available in the boat supply catalogs, including propeller and bubbler systems that run on house current. All are efficient, but my neighbor Bob Mason made up his own de-icer from surplus parts gathered up around his shop, and it works great!

Retired engineer Bob is a tinkerer who never throws anything away. So, he has plenty of parts from just about everything to make just about anything.

To protect his sailboat from winter ice at his dock, he came up with an ingenious solution. An air conditioning compressor from an old Dodge was mated to a one-horsepower 220-volt electric motor and mounted on a board. The motor is controlled by a thermostat set below freezing that operates a low voltage power-handling relay. The rig sits outside his house under a plastic tub.

Instead of running the power line to the dock with an associated electric power loss, he pumps the air through the underground water supply pipe from the house to the dock. There, compressed air goes to a weighted perforated pipe lying on the bottom around his boat. A hard freeze closes the thermostat which powers the compressor that pumps air to the perforated pipe around the sailboat hull. Bubbles circulate warmer bottom water upward to melt ice forming around the boat.

Bob used a regular bubbler hose made for the purpose around his boat. One could also use a vinyl garden soaker hose and tie heavy fishing sinkers every foot along it to keep it from floating.

TEMPORARY BOAT DOCK

I saw this clever temporary boat dock on a lake in New Brunswick, Canada. It seemed like a great solution to winter ice damage. Just pull the dock up on dry land in late fall, then reposition it after ice-out in the spring.

A pair of wheels on an axle from a wrecked vehicle can be mounted on a U-shaped bracket and bolted to the end of the "dock" to provide mobility. Pipes driven in the ground at water's edge are joined by a cross bar to support the beach end of the dock. A sloping ramp secured to the driven pipes provides access across beach mud.

DOCK LINE PULLEY TO HELP BOARDING

The addition of a 1/2" capacity galvanized pulley (white arrow in photo below) with a flat mounting surface was secured with two 5" long galvanized lag bolts to the starboard mooring piling in a vertical position. This allows the portside stern of my 22-foot outboard hull to be pulled close enough to the dock for easy boarding.

The starboard stern mooring line was attached to the boat's stern cleat and threaded through the pulley, then secured at its end to a cleat on the dock piling.

The boat can be secured in its moored position by pulling the starboard line until the boat is centered in its space, then the line is secured to the cleat on the dock piling. When the boat needs to be next to the dock for boarding, the line on the piling cleat is loosened and enough slack is allowed so the boat comes close to, but does not touch the dock. The portside stern dock line is wrapped around a cleat fastened to the dock boards (black arrow in above photo) to restrain it close to the dock.

In areas of high winds or long fetches across big waters, I would not recommend this system—especially for boats much over 20 feet!

SMALL BOAT ROLLER RAMP

Photo by C. Boyd Pfeiffer

This novel boat conveyer was used to move boats around a dam in Louisiana. It may have been made commercially.

It struck me that a similar rig could be made to beach small boats on lakes or even tidal waters if the tide range is not too great —or if the beach doesn't have a steep slope.

A possible way to build such a ramp would include 2 x 6 in. or 2 x 8 in. treated lumber for side rails, large diameter galvanized pipe screwed into pipe flanges at both ends, and pieces of PVC pipe slipped over the galvanized pipe for rollers. Some way of anchoring the ramp for high water conditions should be utilized.

The leaning position of the angler in the above photo indicates he should get some help so he doesn't hurt his back!

SNOOK LIGHTS FOR STRIPERS

Florida anglers often fish after dark under "snook lights" at the end of docks. Lights directed into the water attract baitfish, or in Florida, shrimp. Snook congregate under the lights to feed.

In Chesapeake Bay waters, lights shined downward from the end of a dock will attract baitfish, which in turn entice stripers.

Get an electrician to rig your "snook light," and make sure the electrical outlet is Ground Fault Circuit Interrupter (GFCI) protected so no one gets an electric shock.

The light must shine down into the water where it is fairly deep, perhaps four to six feet at the end of the dock. Leave it on from just after dark for about three hours every night—when the snook feed in Florida, or from May to October on Chesapeake Bay.

Flies or small lures that mimic baitfish cast into the breaking fish under the light will almost always result in strikes.

TIDE INDICATOR

Ed Schartner made this tide gauge/indicator in the 1960s, and I told him he should have patented the ingenious device.

The lower pipe is white PVC, and the upper clear pipe fits into the lower pipe via a machined adaptor. The bottom is open to allow water to raise a weighted float. The top is open so air isn't trapped inside. The lower end of the bottom pipe that is submerged in tidal waters most of the time is coated with an antifouling paint to ward off barnacles and oysters.

Connecting the bottom weight/float and the upper (white) tide-height indicator is a stainless steel rod. The red button (see arrow)

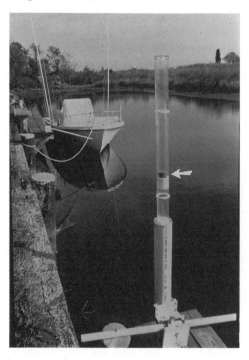

inside the upper indicator is spring-loaded to provide friction against the interior of the clear tube so it will pop up when the tide starts to ebb; it disappears into the white indicator when the tide is rising. The red button is captive in the white indicator so it will only move upward three-quarters of its length. Some details need to be worked out by the skilled craftsman who wants to build one of these units. I've never seen one on the market.

The unit is mounted high enough on the dock so it can be seen from the house. Two exterior sliding white rings on the clear pipe indicate the high-low range of tides. The entire unit is bracketed to the dock with U-bolts to adjust for tidal ranges.

When the red button can be seen, it tells the boater the tide is ebbing, and his shallow creek entrance will soon be too shoal for navigation. When the red button is hidden inside the upper white indicator, the tide is flooding.

Annual maintenance consists of removing the unit so winter ice won't destroy it, and periodic cleaning.

• • • • • • • • • • • • • • •

ROPE AND PULLEY TIE-OUT

One of the simplest ways to tie out a small boat is to drive a stake or pipe in the bottom where there is enough water to float the craft, and add a pulley near the top of it facing the shore.

A continuous loop of rope between the pulley and shore with a short dropper attached to the bow of the boat, and another dropper attached to the stern makes it easy to bring the boat in.

This can be a temporary rig while a permanent dock is being built, or semipermanent in protected waters. It is not recommended for open waters with a long fetch across them where high winds can build high seas and do considerable damage.

BOAT DOCK FISHING BENCH

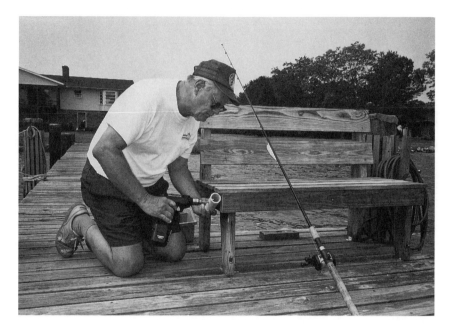

In the photograph above the author installs PVC pipe rod holders on his dock bench with a cordless drill (safety first!) and stainless steel square-drive screws.

The bench is made from treated lumber in three sizes: 2 x 6 in. uprights and legs, a 2 x 4 in. "box" frame to support the seat and tie in with the legs, and 1 x 6 in. seat and seat back. Galvanized 16-penny nails were used to tie the box frame and legs together. Galvanized roofing nails secured the seat bottom and back to the box frame and uprights.

Not visible in the center of the back of the box frame is a galvanized eye bolt with a diameter slightly larger than the pipe of a table umbrella. The umbrella pipe slides through the eye bolt, and its base is seated in the 2 x 4 in. block nailed to the dock decking, visible just behind and under the seat.

The bench is secured to the dock's decking boards with galvanized L-brackets and stainless steel square-drive screws.

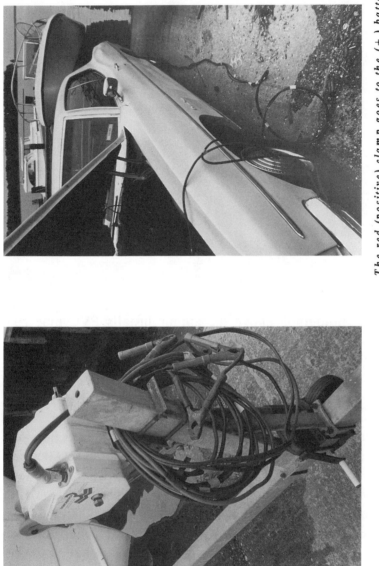

The red (positive) clamp goes to the (+) battery terminal first and the black (-) clamp is secured to the metal bumper last for safety.

The combination cable after picking up the boat.

COMBINED JUMPER & ELECTRIC WINCH CABLE

An inexpensive homemade cable assembly can serve the angler as both a jumper cable and a boat trailer electric winch cable. It can be a car-to-car or boat-to-boat jumper cable: Adding an electric winch plug and wire kit makes it a boat trailer electric winch cable that can be moved from one tow vehicle to another. The total length of my jumper/winch cable is 27 feet: 21 feet for the jumper cables, and a six-foot power winch cable extension that is soldered to one end of the jumper cables.

I assembled my 21-foot jumper cables by soldering a black handled battery cable clamp to each end of a 21-foot length of black insulated 4-gauge copper wire, and soldering a red handled clamp to each end of a 21 foot length of red insulated 4-gauge wire. All surfaces to be soldered were cleaned with steel wool, and after the wires were clamped firmly into the handles, the joints to be soldered were heated until the resin core solder melted and flowed into the junction. A wrap of electrical tape every foot or so along the entire length keeps the two cables together and tangle-free.

My electric winch wiring kit consisted of a plug to fit into the power socket of the winch attached to a double cable of number six copper wire. The black (-) negative conductor, about six feet long, was soldered to the black battery clamp at one end of the jumper cable. Observing proper polarity is important. The longer of the two electric winch wires (red) was cut off even with the black one, and the small cans containing the winch circuit breakers were soldered between the red positive (+) power winch wire and the red jumper cable clamp.

Next, I checked the combined cable's polarity by connecting the polarized plug to the power winch and connecting the opposite end of the jumper cables to a 12-volt car battery, positive (red) clamp to positive (+) battery terminal, and negative (black) clamp to the negative (-) battery terminal. With the winch switched on, the cable wound properly over the top of the drum.

In use, the trailer is backed into the launching ramp before the jumper/winch cable is hooked up. After the power cable plug is inserted into the winch receptacle, the jumper/winch cables are extended on the ground to the front of the tow vehicle.

⚠ **It is very important to keep the red and black unused jumper cable clamps near the back of the vehicle separated** by clamping one of them to the insulated cover of the opposite wire. Don't let the rear red clamp touch the car!

After raising the car's hood, the red clamp is attached to the positive (+) post of the car's battery. Then, as recommended by auto safety experts, the black cable clamp is attached to the auto's metal bumper or frame at some distance from the battery to prevent sparks that could result in injury from an exploding battery.

● ● ● ● ● ● ● ● ● ● ● ● ● ● ● ●

COMBINATION TRAILER DOLLY/SPARE TIRE

In 1987, I attended the Minnesota Inventor's Congress and saw this combination trailer dolly/spare tire. I thought it had great merit, but I didn't get the inventor's name. The idea may now be patented.

While I do not recommend copying a patented invention, it may now be available in boating catalogs.

TRAILER HOOKUP MIRROR

Backing the tow vehicle to your boat trailer tongue can be chancy if no one is around to guide you.

There are several trailer alignment devices on the market including a pair of fiberglass rods, one each attached to the car and trailer. One could make such a set from old fishing rods.

But, I found that a low cost truck rearview mirror attached to the winch stand on my trailer serves the same purpose. Once properly adjusted so I can see the mirror on the trailer, either over my shoulder or in my station wagon's rearview mirror, I carefully back up until the trailer's hitch receiver is over the ball on the wagon's hitch.

The mounting bracket that came with the mirror was adapted to fit under the U-bolt that holds the trailer winch's bracket. Once adjusted, the saltwater exposure soon rusted the mirror's ball-and-socket joint in place.

LAUNCH RAMP SAFETY CHOCKS

Photos of cars that were launched with boats make many anglers nervous at a steep ramp. They wonder if their tow vehicle's emergency brake will hold while their boat is launched or retrieved.

Many of us who trailer our boats regularly use a set of chocks behind the vehicle's rear wheels when launching or retrieving.

You often see chocks used by utility workers when they park their trucks to work on telephone or power lines—even if the truck is on level ground! You can copy their chocks, or make your own. Their chocks usually have a short loop of rope attached for easy removal. This is impractical on a boat ramp because the chocks must be removed before retrieving the boat so the trailer doesn't run over them, negating the safety aspect of the chocks.

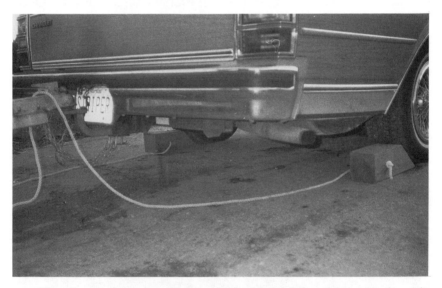

Chocks can be made from a 24" piece of 6 x 6 in. wood cut in half at a 45-degree angle to make two equal pieces. Drill a 1/2" hole through each chock to accommodate 3/8" rope. Make the rope long enough to extend from one chock across the trailer hitch to the opposite chock, but short enough so the chocks drag along out of reach of the trailer's wheels when retrieving the boat.

TURNBUCKLE-UP FOR SAFETY

A galvanized turnbuckle attached between my boat and trailer has provided me with an extra measure of safety while trailering and lets me remove my Powerwinch® when the boat is in storage.

First, I installed a 1/2" diameter galvanized eye bolt on the trailer's winch stand upright. This eye bolt is the attachment point for one end of the turnbuckle.

My turnbuckle has a U-shaped clevis or shackle at each end and is a minimum of 13" long when the two 1/2" diameter threaded screws are fully retracted. I replaced the two clevis or shackle pins in each end with 3/8" dia. x 2" long stainless cap screws. Nylock nuts were used on the cap screws so over-the-road vibration wouldn't loosen them.

The boat is winched tightly against the bow stop roller on the trailer and one clevis is bolted to the bow eye of the boat and the other to the eye bolt on the trailer. Then, I tighten the turnbuckle.

The extra measure of safety provided by the turnbuckle is reassuring while trailering, but that is not the only reason I use it. Not only is my Powerwinch® out of the weather during the winter, it is locked up out of sight when the boat is unattended at a ramp or motel.

TRAILER WALKBOARD

The author hooking up the Mako to load it on the trailer.

Adding a walkboard to a boat trailer can make the boat loading process safer and easier.

The walkboard for my Mako's trailer was a piece of 1 x 12 in. pine shelving eight feet long which matched the flat areas on the trailer cross braces and spanned four of them. This allowed me to climb onto the board at the tongue end of the trailer and kept my feet dry when the wheel hubs were just out of the water.

Before I installed my walkboard, both sides of it were rolled with white exterior latex paint. While the paint was wet I sprinkled some dry sand on the upper side to give the walking surface some "tooth" to prevent me from slipping and falling.

To attach the walkboard to the trailer, I used 3/8" diameter stainless steel cap screws with washers on the upper side and a stainless steel washer and stainless steel Nylock nuts on the underside.

Before walking to the rear of the trailer along the board, I locked the latch that keeps the trailer tongue from tilting. The hook end of the winch cable was carried with me as I walked along the board to hook it to the bow eye of the boat.

Some boat trailers will not accommodate a walkboard. My walkboards were easy to install. The additional safety and the easier loading of my boat was worth the minimal effort and expense.

• • • • • • • • • • • • • • •

JON-BOAT EASY LOADER

Loading an aluminum skiff or jon boat into the back of a pickup truck can be made easier by the simple installation of a boat trailer roller on the truck's tailgate.

Jack Stovall bolted a boat trailer roller purchased from a marine supply store a few inches from the end of the tailgate of his pickup. It is easy for him to lift one end of his (unloaded) 14-foot aluminum skiff onto the end of the tailgate and slide the boat as far as it will go toward the front of the truck's bed. There is plenty of room alongside the skiff for the outboard motor and tackle. Some states require that a red flag be tied to anything extending more than a foot or two behind the vehicle. Check your local laws about this.

Unloading the boat at your favorite fishing hole goes easier with two men, but a lone angler can still handle a lightweight skiff with the roller's help. Simply skid the boat to the shoreline, add motor and tackle and push off. The procedure is reversed for picking up the skiff.

TRAILER LOADING LIGHT

Those who pursue fish that bite best from late afternoon until after dark will, of course, return to the launching ramp and load their boats on trailers in the dark.

Many of these anglers install a 12-volt lamp under their electric winch to make loading the boat easier, and safer, after dark. These 12-volt lamps can be purchased in auto parts or marine supply stores.

It is simple to drill an appropriate hole in the winch stand near the power winch to mount the light, and wire it directly to the power leads inside the winch. Make sure the light is not wired so it operates with the power winch switch, or the lamp will only come on when the winch is switched on. You want the lamp to be lit when the power winch cord is plugged into the winch.

This simple addition to a power winch can make the evening angler's life a little easier at boat loading time—and safer.

TRACTOR HITCH TO MOVE BOATS

Those who are lucky enough to have a farm tractor with a hydraulic three-point hitch can rig it to move their trailered boat around the yard for maintenance or to mow the area where it is normally parked.

You can buy a heavy duty steel crossbar with several 3/4" diameter holes that attaches between the two lower lift arms. Check with your tractor dealer for the proper equipment. I fastened my crossbar ends with bolts and Nylock nuts for security, instead of using the standard ring clips that can come loose. I mounted one 2" trailer hitch ball and one 1-7/8" hitch ball on the crossbar.

Since the cross-bar can rotate and decouple the ball from the trailer receiver, I bolted a piece of 1-1/2" square bar stock between the crossbar and one three-point hitch lift arm as a stabilizer.

⚠ Caution! Before attaching ANY three-point hitch implement be sure any necessary weights are added and correctly distributed on the tractor for safe operation and stability! Front frame weights, wheel weights, and rear wheel weights are available. When lifting a heavy trailer, make sure you have adequate balance weights on the tractor. Use only implements and weights that are approved for that tractor. When moving boat trailers with this hitch system, lock the trailer ball in place. Also, use a low tractor gear and go slowly. On sloping ground, make sure you block trailer wheels securely before disconnecting the tractor so the trailer won't roll.

⚠ NEVER place your body or any body parts between the tractor and trailer or their parts at any time! Behave like the equipment will hurt you if it can, because if you don't, it will!

• • • • • • • • • • • • • • • •

TRAILERING TIPS

Before towing your boat on the open road, make a visual check of your rig:

• Check all tire pressures with a gauge, including the spare. The maximum tire pressure is molded into the sidewall of the trailer's tires.

• Check the trailer ball and safety chains. Chains should be crisscrossed under the trailer tongue to support the trailer in case you hit a bump and the hitch ball and coupler disconnect. Make sure the hitch coupler's locking lever is in the down position, the ball is locked to the coupler, and a pin or padlock is on the locking lever.

• Make sure the winch cable is tight with the boat's bow against the stop. A safety chain should be connected between the boat's bow towing eye and the trailer to keep the boat from jumping over the winch stand. A strap or other tie-downs should be tight at the boat's stern to keep the boat and trailer together in case of a panic stop.

• Raise the outboard motor or I/O lower unit to the towing position and lock it in place. Some motors use a separate motor brace for towing.

• Make sure all the drain plugs are installed in your boat.

• Prepare for launching before leaving home to avoid conflict at the launch ramp. Place all tackle, coolers, and other gear aboard the boat and attach lines to the bow and stern cleats for launching and docking. Secure everything so it won't blow out of the boat underway, or fall overboard when launching.

• Tongue weight is generally about 10 percent of the total loaded weight of the boat and trailer. Not enough weight on the tongue can cause the boat to fishtail at highway speeds and cause an accident. Too much weight on the tongue overloads the rear of the tow car and the hitch. Follow the trailer manufacturer's instructions.

• Check the springs and axle for excess rust. I found several broken spring leaves on one of my trailers, which prompted me to replace springs, attaching bolts, axle, and bearings. One friend bent his trailer axle by crossing a ditch too soon, and found it was rusted almost through and could have let him down on the open road.

• Check wheel bearings and if they are worn, replace them before getting on the road. Add wheel bearing lubricators if you don't have them. Make a visual inspection of the grease in the clear plastic hub and add lubricant if necessary.

• Check brake and directional signal lights before you leave home. Ask your partner to stand behind the trailer as you try directional signals and brakes and report if they are working. Replace burned-out bulbs, and make sure trailer plug contacts are free from corrosion.

• If the trailer is equipped with brakes, check their adjustment according to the owner's manual, and make sure the breakaway lanyard is connected, with enough slack for tight turns.

• License plate holders on boat trailers are subject to theft, wear, tear, and corrosion. Make sure the license plate is still in place.

• Adjust the pressure in air-adjustable shock absorbers so that the boat trailer and tow vehicle are level.

• Powerwinch® sells a stud kit to replace the three bolts that hold their winch on the trailer winch stand. These studs fit the keyhole-shaped slots on the bottom of the winch. Once the studs are properly fitted to your winch stand, place the winch on the stand using the keyhole slots, and use a Nylock nut and bolt in the matching hole between stand and winch to make sure the winch doesn't slip. This allows you to remove the winch at boat ramps while you are out fishing and store it in the car trunk out of sight, and also to remove it for winter storage.

• Consider replacing trailer bunks when necessary with treated 2 x 6 in. or 2 x 4 in. lumber. It will out last the untreated boards. Teflon® strips are better than carpet because they have less friction, but be sure to recess the nail heads.

• When your boat is off the trailer, consider greasing or lightly oiling the trailer rollers for easier launching.

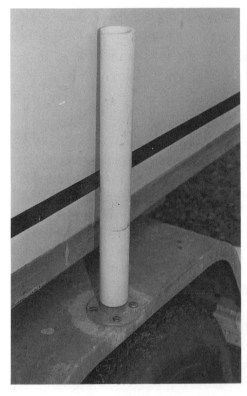

PVC Boat Positioner

• Trailer guide-ons didn't work for my 22-foot boat. No matter what I did the boat was never centered on the trailer when retrieving.

My solution was to install a boat positioner made from 1" i.d. galvanized pipe nipple 10" long, threaded into a pipe flange and attached to one trailer fender with stainless steel bolts and Nylock nuts. A 12" piece of 1-1/4" i. d. PVC pipe fits over the galvanized pipe as a hull protector/roller.

While the boat is on the trailer in the water, a buddy stands on the boat's portside with a boat hook and a short line and adjusts the hull so it is about an inch from the PVC positioner. My solution may not be sanctioned by boat or trailer manufacturers, but it works for me.

Be secure in the knowledge you have checked everything in your control. Drive defensively when towing—remember to add distance to the interval between you and the car ahead, because the extra weight of your towed rig adds to your stopping distance.

ANCHORING FOR ANGLERS

In recent years, chumming for stripers, weakfish, and croaker have become popular. But, if you want to see a disaster about to happen, watch the chumming fleet on a windy day. Anchors continually break loose and boats drift down wind toward others whose anchors are holding. It's like watching a train wreck about to happen. There is nothing you can do but watch, and hope the drifters soon learn more about anchoring before they hurt someone.

I have used a nine-pound 8S **Danforth anchor** since 1974 on two boats: A 20-foot Mako center console outboard hull, and lately a 22-foot walkaround cuddy outboard. On the Mako, I attached a sash weight about six feet above the anchor with a large galvanized snap. I didn't

want to store a heavy, rusty chain. In moderate holding conditions, a sash weight snapped to the anchor rode can be a temporary solution. The sash weight lies on the bottom like a piece of chain above the anchor and supplies horizontal pull to dig the anchor's flukes into the bottom. I still use 150 feet of 1/2-inch nylon rope as the rode, but on the newer boat I have a six-foot length of heavy galvanized chain attached to the 8S Danforth anchor.

I am always concerned about a fishing buddy going forward to pull anchor in sloppy seas. So, I've tried several ways to pull anchor and stay amidships.

In the Florida Keys, a friend pulled anchor by starting his motor and idling off to one side until he was clear of the rode (he thought), and then motoring upwind. Unfortunately, he ran across the rode; it wrapped around his I/O lower unit and killed his motor. The boat swung around, stern to the wind. Waves came over the transom. We finally got the rode unwrapped, but that situation was doubly scary because the other fishing boats had left for the day and we were alone. I do not recommend this system!

A variation on that idea is often used offshore. A float ball with a large snap (available from most marine supply stores) is clipped over the anchor rode outboard of the bow cleat. The boat moves ahead until the anchor pulls out of the bottom. When the anchor rode has pulled all the way through the large snap ring, the anchor engages the ring. Then the floating anchor is retrieved safely aboard into the after cockpit. But, again, there is the possibility the rode can wrap around the propeller. Scary!

I use a variation on the last two systems. If it might be rough where I plan to fish, I get the anchor out of the bow compartment in calm water. I then tie off a suitable length of rode to the bow cleat. The anchor and a 5 to 1 scope of rode (rode 150 feet for a depth of 30 feet) are secured aft in the cockpit. Then, I snap a 20-foot length of "slider" line over the rode outboard of the bow rail and tie the other end to the after end of the bow rail at the cockpit. When setting or retrieving the anchor in rough water, no one needs to go forward. It takes two to retrieve the anchor with this system. One to run the boat ahead and to one side of the rode very slowly as the other person, safe in the aft cockpit, takes in line as the snap slides down the rode toward the anchor. When 20 feet or less of the "slider" line is in, the anchor rode is in the puller's hands.

⚠ Communication must be good between the captain and the anchor-puller so the rode never gets near the propeller.

You often see watermen's workboats anchored from the stern (not recommended for small boats). You will also notice their anchor rode is almost vertical! How do they do that? They use a **grappling hook-style anchor** with five flukes flattened on the ends to dig into the bottom. A length of chain is sometimes added.

One version of the grappling anchor (above), used by charter Captain Mike Haddaway of Bozman, MD, has a ring at the base of the anchor for a "trip line." Mike often fishes the Airplane Wreck in the mouth of the Choptank River. If he gets hung up in the wreck, no problem. His trip line has a float he can haul aboard and un-toggle his anchor from the wreck.

Several years ago, I took divers to the Airplane Wreck. This is not a place for amateur divers—jagged metal and fish hooks are everywhere. These chaps were pros. However, the line they rigged between our two boats caused my Danforth anchor to slip and toggle into the wreck. Since the divers used my anchor line as a vertical highway to the wreck, it was no problem for them to bring it up on their last dive. But the wreck is decorated with lots of anchors, so there must be another way. There is—a **wreck anchor.**

Consider two versions of **wreck or rockpile** anchors: **Rebar** and **aluminum-tined** with a lead-loaded stock. The rebar and the aluminum-tined are designed to bend. Rebar anchors are made of 3/8" or 1/2" steel reinforcing rod, available from hardware stores. Four or five tines are welded together with a ring at the top for the anchor rode. A coat of paint keeps them from rusting and staining the boat. In use, the rebar anchor is toggled into a wreck or rockpile. If it won't come loose when it's time to leave, the tines can be pulled straight with boat power. Tines are easily rebent.

⚠ Stay out of the way of a possibly breaking stretched line.

This Mighty-Mite anchor's stock fits down through a hole in the top of the anchor locker so the tines rest down on the top of the locker for safety.

Aluminum tines on the new **15-pound Mighty-Mite wreck/ rock anchor** are easily rebent, too. It has five 5/16" aluminum bar stock tines, sharpened at the ends so they will hold in soft or hard bottom in addition to rocks and wrecks. The main difference in this anchor is that the tines and top ring are secured inside a 1-1/2" i. d. aluminum pipe filled with lead. No chain is needed with this anchor, its maker says, because its stock is so heavy. This anchor is not tossed, but lowered slowly to the bottom. You don't want to toss it at a rockpile, either, since it is front-loaded the stock will hit the rocks before the tines. Result: a lost anchor.

Those who chum the Chesapeake Bay Bridge pilings or rock piles want precise placement of chum and/or bait in certain eddy currents. You will often see a combination of anchors used here; two Danforths or grappling anchors set in a "Vee" from the bow, and a rebar anchor is toggled into a rock pile. This allows precision placement of the boat by adjusting anchor rodes.

A small **navy anchor** (above) on a short rode (20 to 25 feet in my case) often comes in handy when fishing in shallow water. When drifting and casting surface plugs in 3 to 5 feet of water, a striped bass or bluefish might announce its presence by striking at the lure. A swirl or splash near the plug, and you want to stay in the area and check it out. Simply slide the small anchor overboard and secure its rode to a cleat. In calm water it will hold you in one place; in moderate winds, it might slide along the bottom, giving you the chance to make a few additional casts.

We've come a long way from the simple **mushroom** or **cinderblock anchors** that we used in small ponds and streams. Chesapeake Bay and other big waters can get rough. Rocks and wrecks often keep expensive anchors, so we look at cheaper alternatives. And high winds sometimes make me wish I'd bought a 13S Danforth anchor instead of the 8S that has served so well.

A DOUBLE BUOY FOR PRECISE ANCHORING

Precise anchoring over a small wreck or obstruction that holds fish can be made easier with the simple addition of a small float on a 6-foot cord tied to your marker buoy.

Captain Mike Murphy of Easton, Maryland carries such a rig on his 25-foot charterboat. When he reaches the spot where his GPS says a fishing spot like the Choptank River's Airplane Wreck is located, he drops his double buoy with enough weight at the end of the cord to keep it in place.

Then, he slowly circles his double buoy until he finds the wreck on his depth sounder. By this time, his double buoy has settled, and the smaller float on a short line off his buoy has swung around with the wind and tide to show him which way his boat will lie at anchor. He simply motors upwind and upcurrent, as dictated by his double buoy, and then he anchors. It's funny, but new arrivals to fish the wreck often anchor next to his original buoy!

If you are lucky enough to get your double buoy (as shown below) directly on top of fish-holding structure, motor upwind or upcurrent of the double buoy keeping the float and the buoy aligned, and drop anchor as far from the buoy as you need anchor rode scope to hold bottom. Then let out enough anchor rode to put you on top of the fish!

ANCHORING TIPS

- Check boating supply catalogs or Charles F. Chapman's Piloting, Seamanship, and Small boat Handling" for the latest anchor and rode recommendations.
- Slow the drift of a small fishing boat by dragging a piece of heavy chain on the end of a rope. The photograph below shows such a drag anchor on the left, with a piece of rope just long enough so the chain won't tangle in the outboard motor's propeller when the boat moves from place to place. A new piece of chain is in the center. A homemade "coffee can" anchor is on the right, made by pouring lead in a tin can and adding an eye bolt.

Photo by C. Boyd Pfeiffer

- An anchor for rocky bottom can be made from an old steel plate used to anchor railroad rails to the wooden ties. Attach it to the anchor rode with a piece of chain for abrasion resistance.

⚠ If you fish downstream of a dam that periodically releases a large flow of water, keep a knife handy to cut the anchor rode if you can't get the plate up when they blow the dam's warning horn!

- Make a wreck anchor with 3/8" rebar reinforcement rod. Bend one 60" piece in half around a piece of pipe to make an eye and put it through an 18" long piece of 1-1/4" i. d. galvanized pipe. Cut two or three more pieces of rebar (as many as you can fit into the pipe), long enough to extend from the eye end of the pipe out the other end far enough to make anchor flukes the same length as the doubled piece. Pour enough epoxy into the pipe to grip the rebar pieces.

⚠ If you block one end of the pipe with a wet rag and pour in lead, wear eye protection and work in a well-ventilated place! Bend the flukes with a three or four foot piece of pipe and keep it handy on board the boat to rebend the rebar after straightening it when pulling the stuck anchor off a wreck. Spray the anchor with aluminum paint.

• Plastic buckets make good emergency sea anchors to keep your bow headed into the wind, or slow your drift while fishing. Tie the bucket to the end of a 50-foot piece of line. If you want to drift broadside, make up a bridle from the bow to stern, then tie the sea anchor's line midway on the bridle with a bowline knot. A bucket towed astern will also slow your trolling speed, but keep the line away from the propeller!

• For shallow-water casting, Sherman Baynard ties a small anchor to one end of a short rode and a 12" piece of wood closet rod to the other end as shown in the above photo. Luckily, one gunwale rod holder is exactly midships on his 17-foot Mako. He places the dowel in that rod holder and drops anchor. His boat lays across the current, allowing one angler to cast from the bow and one from the stern.

• If you want to chase big fish, but you are anchored and want to return to the same spot, secure an adequate length of anchor rode to a float, with enough extra rode to reach the bow cleat. Simply untie the rode and toss it over, chase the fish, and return to your old position. Other anglers snap a short piece of line to the float and tie it to the cleat. Another more complicated system assumes you can reach the bow eye of your boat; put a loop of line through the bow eye and make another loop with the float end of your rode. Slip that loop through the first loop. When you want to chase a fish, simply pull on the float. The last loop will pull out of the first one and you can toss the marker buoy overboard to chase your fish.

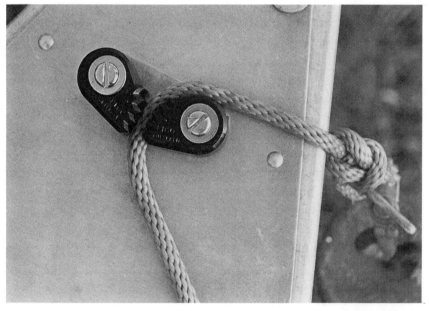

Photo by C. Boyd Pfeiffer

• As shown above, a sailboater's cam cleat mounted on the bow of an aluminum boat. The "coffee can" lead anchor's rode is temporarily suspended from the cam cleat. By pulling on the rode, the cam cleat opens so the angler can drop anchor. Then, the rode is allowed to ride against one side of the cam cleat as more line is fed out, closing the cleat.

Lay thread end over

Come around one time

Form a locking x

A few more turns

Trim loose ends

Install pull thru loop

Complete the wrap

Run line thru loop

Pull both tight

Pull loop thru

All the way thru

Trim loose end

Drawings courtesy of Gudebrod.

RODS ——————————————

REPLACING ROD GUIDES AND TIP-TOPS

A broken rod guide or tip can easily be replaced by the home craftsman. To replace a guide, gather up a few tools and materials: A rod guide that matches the broken one, thread (more on this later), scissors, single edge razor blade, a two-part epoxy rod finish, and masking tape, plus a simple rod winding lathe like the one in the next section "Inexpensive Rod Winding Lathe."

Thread comes in many sizes and colors. Try to match the thread color on the remaining of your guide wraps on your rod. This is not always possible, but thread manufacturer Gudebrod lists 33 different colors, available from most tackle shops. Most thread manufacturers recommend using a color preserver on the thread after wrapping. If you use preserver, let it dry thoroughly before applying the epoxy rod finish. (The "N.C.P." specification in the tackle supply catalog means "No Color Preserver" needed).

Thread sizes recommended for various rods:

"00" for fly rods and ultralight freshwater rods
"A" for light saltwater and most freshwater spin and
     casting rods
"D" for freshwater - medium to heavy
     light-action saltwater spin and casting rods
     saltwater fly rods
"E" for average saltwater surf and trolling rods

Note: Most rods will use size "A." This writer uses "E" for everything including bucktail jig-making. It's a little heavy for most rod guide uses, but it simplifies my inventory.

The drawings on the opposite page, courtesy of Gudebrod, illustrate how to wrap a new or replacement guide on a rod. Heavy-duty trolling or surf rods should get one layer of underwrap before installing the guide. For more detail on rod building, consult the publications and vendors listed in the Bibliography.

Once the guide has been wrapped on the rod, apply the recommended color preserver to the thread and let it dry. Then, mix the two-part clear epoxy and apply it evenly to cover the thread. The epoxy will run before it sets up, and form an ugly glob on the lowest point of the rod. **To avoid this, immediately after coating, slowly rotate the rod until the epoxy sets up.** I use epoxy with a 5-minute setup time for this reason. If the expert advice in a manufacturer's book doesn't agree with my system, follow theirs and you can't go wrong. They know their products. So far, clear 5-minute epoxy has worked for me.

A broken or chipped rod tip is easily replaced. To remove the old tip, carefully apply low heat to soften the heat-setting cement and remove the tip gently. If you use too much heat, the tip of the rod itself can be damaged. I have done this—the tip became mushy, and drooped over. There was no option but to cut off the soft part of the tip and use a larger diameter replacement tip, which did not noticeably change the rod's action.

To install a new tip, first heat the end of a stick of ferrule cement and apply it to the end of the rod. Before the cement sets up, slide the new tube-type tip on the rod and adjust it to align with the rod guides. When the cement hardens, carefully peel away the excess on the rod shaft. Epoxy can be substituted for ferrule cement if necessary.

Heat the ferrule cement   *Apply to the rod shaft*   *Heat the tip guide*

Drawings courtesy of Gudebrod.

Replacing rod guides and tip-tops can be so much fun, the reader might be tempted to build a custom rod from components. Many fancy touches like diamond wraps and initials can be added by the home craftsman. A complete set of matching rods can be built for the angler's boat in colors matching his tackle box, boat, trailer, and tow car. It has been done. You may decide to go into the rod business. Repairing that first rod can be addictive. Beware!

• • • • • • • • • • • • • • • •

INEXPENSIVE ROD WINDING LATHE

Anglers who have only an occasional need to refurbish a favorite rod or replace a damaged guide can make a handy rod winding lathe from a pair of inexpensive Stanley Number H-157, 6-inch C-Clamps and a set of four nylon casters.

My caster wheels were 1-1/2" in diameter with a swiveling shank, although any casters up to 3" or 4" diameter can be used.

To assemble the two holders that make the rod winding lathe, first attach the C-clamp to the workbench top with the longer standard facing up. Then, hold the caster wheels in place, one on each side of the C-clamp standard so you can mark the caster side plates and the standard for drilling. Make sure the outside radius of the casters overlap to provide a shallow "V" in which to rest the rod under repair.

Then, drill a small hole in each caster side plate and a matching hole in the C-clamp standard. A small nut and bolt will hold everything together. A piece of tape around the shank of the caster will keep the caster shafts aligned. Make two of these C-clamp rod holders—one to support each end of the rod being repaired.

In use, the rod holders are clamped to the edge of a workbench or table with the caster wheels facing upward and about three or four feet apart, depending on the length of the rod under repair. A rod placed in the "V" formed by the casters will be held in a comfortable working position and can easily be rotated by hand.

For infrequent repairs, rod winding thread can be tensioned by feeding it through the pages of a telephone book, but serious rod rebuilders will want to use a thread-tension vise available from mail order tackle suppliers.

A more elaborate rod-winding lathe can be made by attaching the same nylon casters to blocks of wood that can be adjusted along a five or six foot piece of 1 x 6 in. shelving board, but then storage is a problem.

I have successfully used my simple rod winding lathe to rewrap rods of all sizes, from ultralight graphites all the way up to an antique 26-ounce bamboo big game rod tip.

The caster and C-clamp rod winding lathe is quickly and inexpensively made, stores easily, and the rod holders can still be used for their original purpose—as C-clamps.

The author with his rod-winding setup on his living room coffee table.

TIP: Position a rotisserie motor shaft under and parallel to the rod. Connect the shaft and rod with rubber bands to rotate the rod slowly while the epoxy sets up.

REPAIRING A BROKEN ROD

Breaking a favorite fishing rod can cause a lot of anguish. You and that old wand have been together through a lot of fishing and you can't bear to toss it out.

Help is on the way with suggestions from one of my fishing buddies, Jack Stovall. He has repaired several of my favorite fish sticks—it looks so easy I might try it the next time I bust a rod.

First, save a few old fishing rods, or ask your friendly tackle shop owner to save a few old rods for you instead of trashing them. Strip off the old guides and save them if they are in good condition. Sections can be cut from these old rods to make repair sleeves for the next rod you break as shown in the photo below.

Stovall first measures the diameters up-rod and down-rod of the break. It helps if you use a micrometer for extreme accuracy, but it's not necessary. Rods are tapered somewhat, so you want to find a section from one of your junk rods that will fit above and below the break on your repairable one.

If the break is nearest the reel seat the rod's inside diameter might be large enough to accommodate an internal splice. This is not likely because rods almost always break near the tip.

The most likely repair, in my personal experience, will require a sleeve on the outside of the rod. Once you have selected a section of the junk rod where the inside diameter of the sleeve equals the outside of the repair area, and done a fit check, you're ready to epoxy. Mix the two-part epoxy (Stovall uses West System®), and apply a thin coat on the inside of the sleeve and the outside of the repair area. Fit the pieces together with the rod guides aligned and wipe off any excess epoxy. Apply a very thin coat of epoxy on the outside of the repair.

To prevent a lopsided glop of epoxy from forming, rotate the rod slowly until the epoxy sets up. Slow-drying epoxies like West may need a long time to set, while a 5-minute epoxy could save you a lot of rod rotating.

If you used a yellow rod sleeve on a black rod, and don't want the repair to stand out like a bandaged thumb, paint the repair to match the rod *after* the epoxy is set up and hard. If the repair happened to be at the previous site of a rod guide, a new guide can be wrapped on over the sleeve.

I notice no difference in the action of my repaired rods, and they have taken their share of fish since the fixing without crunching or creaking.

ROD TIPS

- Ready-rigged fly rods often won't fit in standard boat rod holders. Upright plastic surface-mount rod holders can be modified to accept a fly rod with a reel attached by sawing a lengthwise slot in the rod holder slightly wider than the width of the fly reel's foot. Be sure and protect the delicate rod tip with foam plastic insulation from beating against a cabin or T-top in a rough seas.

- When transporting several rods that are ready-rigged to fish with a lure's hook engaged in a rod guide, keep them from tangling together by wrapping the length of line between the tip top and the lure once around the rod and securing it around a rod guide. Hard to explain, but easy once you try it. Once you get the hang of it, and use the system, your gear won't wrap itself together in a tight bundle that takes time to unravel. Or, you could cover each rigged rod with a section of foam pipe insulation.

- It is often recommended that older rod guides and tip tops (and on modern ceramic guides) be checked for grooves by pulling a piece of a woman's nylon stocking through them to test for snags. This is an excellent idea, but guides and tip tops can also be checked by close visual inspection as in the photograph below. This badly chipped rod tip escaped detection until it began to fray one of the new superlines.

• For those who don't like to hang lure hooks in a guide for fear of damaging the ceramic, loop a rubber band through the guide and attach the lure to that. Or, simply hang the lure's hook in the guide's bridge.

• Keep a small bottle of clear fingernail polish in your tackle box in case rod windings become frayed while you're on a trip.

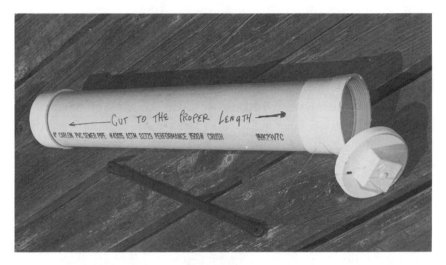

• Rugged rod cases can be easily made from PVC pipe and fittings. Several rods can be packed in a case made from 4 inch diameter thin-wall septic drainfield pipe assuming they will be transported in the angler's vehicle. But, when traveling on airlines or other public transportation, make the rod case from stronger, thick wall Schedule 40 PVC pipe. After measuring the longest rod you plan to use, add an inch or two for packing (I use an old sheet intertwined around the rods), and cut the pipe to length. Using PVC cement, glue a solid pipe cap to one end of the pipe. I glued a threaded clean-out fitting with a screw-in plug to the opposite end of the pipe. This plug can be made captive by drilling a small hole in it and another hole nearby in the rod case, and attaching it with 100-pound test mono leader. Make a carrying handle out of nylon rope or a "Rubber-snubber" tied around the case at each end and securely taped in place.

• Roller guides need constant attention. Trolling rod maintenance is often delegated to the first mate on a charter boat— roller guides are checked before each offshore trip. Rollers must roll, or else line can become abraded and weakened, and a possible record fish lost. Although modern aluminum oxide or silicon carbide ring guides have replaced roller guides on many trolling rods, roller guides are still popular for wire line, and roller tip tops are still used on many light tackle and big game rods. Constant maintenance is the price of success. Disassemble the roller guides, clean off the caked salt with soap and water, then lubricate the roller surfaces.

• One recent lightweight roller guide is designed for IGFA line tests from 2 to 20 pounds. Its single foot is mounted on the rod facing the butt. It is used mainly on casting and light-duty trolling rods. Light-tackle anglers find that roller guides cause less friction (longer casts) and less line abrasion on very light lines (less chance to lose a fish). Anglers who use wind-on leaders to get a fish closer to the boat might pay particular attention to their knots, since these small roller guides have a smaller aperture. A small dab of Teflon® Gel lubricates the guide's rollers.

• If you lose a rod overboard and the water is too deep to see it, first toss a weighted buoy at the spot. Then open a fish stringer's snaps (or tie on a series of blunted treble hooks) and drag the array across the bottom on a fishing line.

• If the rod ferrules are stuck, the way old-timers take a rod apart still works: Grip the stubborn rod horizontally behind your knees with both hands and move your knees apart. This gives you a straight pull and more leverage. Try not to twist the rod. Metal ferrules should be cleaned and lubricated by wiping a bit of oil from the side your nose on the male ferrule before reassembly.

• Small light sticks or tiny bells on the tip of a surf rod make good bite detectors at night. Also, the space between two rod guides near the tip top could also be covered with luminous tape or paint so one could see rod movement in the dark.

• One rod maker designed a rod with several light emitting diodes (LEDs) imbedded along the length of the blank. The batteries and a switch were in the handle. Midnight anglers would not only know just where and what their rod was doing, but they would be treated to a dazzling display of lights similar to the fourth of July!

• Two other rod makers were competing to get first dibs on a "variable action" rod. If an angler doesn't like a wimpy rod, the competing rod designers opined, he could adjust it to pool-cue stiffness in a heartbeat with a twist of the handle. One designer's solution was to put hydraulic fluid in the core of the rod so it could be "loaded" differently. The other maker was going to change the distance between a "rod within a rod." Think of the entertainment value on a dull fishing day if you had a combined "line-of-lights" and "variable stiffness" rod!

• Jack Stovall (above on left, measuring his grandson Henner's spotted seatrout) has a handy fish ruler right on his fishing rod. Stovall painted lines an inch apart on his favorite rod above the reel seat. Saves digging around in the tackle box for a ruler when in doubt—or if there is a cash pool on the longest fish.

- To store long rods on a garage or basement ceiling, I used six-inch long screw hooks, and bent the "hook" part wider to accommodate rod handles. The garage ceiling has wallboard on it, so it was easy to lay out the pattern of the rod hangers. I found the joists above the wallboard and drew light pencil lines 48" apart on the ceiling to indicate the joists above. These were far enough apart to support most rods, two hooks to a rod.

Fishing rods hung from screw hooks in the garage ceiling.

Then, I made tic marks 8" apart along each line for the screw hooks. This spacing works well for even the largest of my reels. I punched small holes through the wallboard to start the hooks, and twisted them in until they were firmly embedded in the joists. Luckily my ceiling height is just right for me to reach up and grab a reel to take the rods down.

- To keep fishing rods from getting tangled, I made a floor-standing rod rack from PVC pipe and some leftover pieces of plastic central vacuum system pipe.

I use the rack when I give talks at shows and to fishing groups. It saves the embarrassment of trying to untangle rods and lines while an impatient audience twiddles its collective thumbs. The same materials could be adapted to just about any space or similar task on your boat or in your garage.

PVC floor-standing rod rack.

I started with a rectangle made from 1" i.d. Schedule 40 PVC pipe as the base. Six "Tees" had an outside diameter that fit the inside diameter of six pieces of 1-5/8" i. d. gray vacuum system pipe that hold the rods vertically. Four 90-degree "Ells" made the corners.

Before assembly, the vacuum pipe was flared on one end by heating it with a paint-peeling heat gun. When the plastic was soft, it was flared over the outside of a large tin funnel.

⚠ Wrap a rag around the pipe and wear heavy gloves as you flare it for safety.

The pipe was glued together with PVC cement.

Hanging rod rack made from old chair back.

• Shorter rods stored in my garage are hung by their eyes on cup hooks. I do not recommend this, and rod manufacturers won't either, but if you're careful you won't damage the tip-tops.

Spacewise, I had no other option but to store them between the garage sink and the well water tank. An old wooden chair back in my junk bin, shaped like an arc, was hung on the wall like an inverted "U" and cup hooks were spaced about 4" apart, screwed into the side facing away from the wall. It holds eight rods, rigged and ready for fishing.

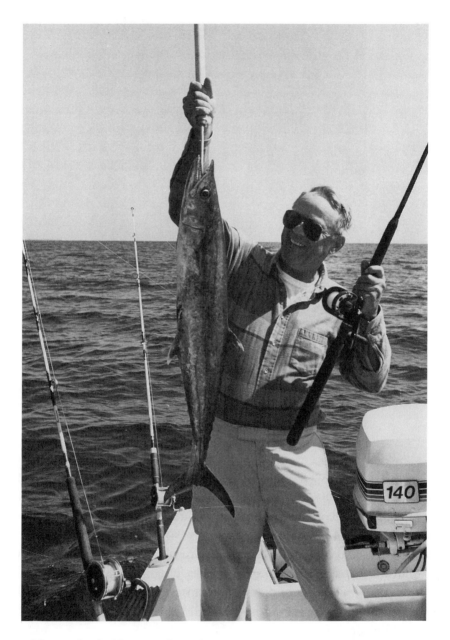

The author's king mackerel is a result of good reel maintenance.

REELS

REEL DRAGS

In 1898, Dr. Charles Fredrick Holder took a tuna weighing 183 pounds off Catalina Island. In the light of today's technologically superior tackle that doesn't seem like a great feat. But, here's the hooker. His reel had a direct drive handle, but no drag. When a fish of that size suddenly pulls on a reel of that vintage the most immediate problem is to get your body parts out of the way of a backward-spinning buzz saw of a handle. The next immediate problem is avoiding a gargantuan backlash. Those minor perplexities taken care of, you have about one nanosecond to decide how many layers of thumb print you are willing to sacrifice to catch a fish. Remember, in those days the only pressure an angler could bring to bear on his tuna was by clamping his thumbs on the reel spool. Even if he had a heavy leather thumbstall he must have had the soul of a Spartan to ignore the heat.

About the turn of the century, William Boschen, working in the cellar workshop of Thomas Conroy's New York tackle store, designed the multiple-disk drag and non-reversing handle that made possible sport-fishing as we know it today. Boschen used a reel incorporating his new design in 1913 to catch the first rod and reel swordfish, effectively stifling those who had ridiculed him. He did not patent his magnificent invention. Not all of us have the opportunity or desire to tangle with a swordfish, but every sport fisherman who has ever heard a reel drag sing owes a debt of gratitude to William Boschen.

Serious tournament anglers set their drags through the bend of the rod, in the fish fighting position. The line is threaded through the guides and tied to a spring scale. A friend holds the scale and calls out the "pounds" drag setting as you back away holding the rod in the fighting position and adjust the drag. This procedure is best done outside. Line "pops" have given me some dandy dents in the living room ceiling to prove it.

Some big-game fishermen recommend a striking drag of about 1/3 of the line test and a fighting drag of about 1/2 of line test. Stiffer rods require a slightly lesser setting than limber ones. Lever drag reels of the Fin-Nor type give the angler the benefit of setting both striking drag and fighting drag and simply moving the lever to change settings.

Most of my reels are not lever drags, however, and I set them to a little less than 1/2 of line test and leave them set there for the season. If a fish manages to take out half the line on a reel the reduced diameter of the line on the spool can double drag tension, and a large amount of line in the water also adds drag. In that case, I scientifically loosen the drag—and cross my fingers.

Rod guide types have a bearing on drag settings. Ring guides offer more friction than roller guides, but roller guides need more maintenance as discussed previously in ROD TIPS. See page 115.

Those of us who have fished for more than three decades have noticed how much smoother reel drags are lately. While alternating leather and steel washers compressed on a spindle or axle were once the backbone of reel drag technology, other materials that are slicker and more heat-resistant are used now. Teflon, felt, stainless steel, aluminum, titanium, cork, and various composites in numerous combinations are finding their way into reel drags lately.

Another interesting development is the dual-drag reel. Shimano's Bait Runner® spinning reels incorporate two separate drag systems. One drag is set lighter for hook-setting when a fish strikes the bait. When the angler reels the handle, the second, heavier drag comes into play for the fight. See top photo on page 123.

Lever drag reels can also be set up for a dual drag situation. By first placing the lever against its stop and setting the fighting drag at about 1/3 line strength, then backing the lever off to about half that for setting the hook as a running fish takes the bait, the angler can then place a mark with a permanent marker on each side of the lever's quadrant plate. That way, the angler has two reliable drag settings—one for hook setting, another for fighting the fish.

Most of us have fished for years using the "Feels-right" school of drag setting, where you pull some line off the spool and adjust the drag until it "feels right." But if we intend to use William Boschen's wonderful invention to its fullest—say to try for the

IGFA's 10-1 Club where the fish caught must weigh 10 times line test—we'd better spend some time tweaking up our reel drags.

The time is now.

*Reels set up for
dual-drag action.*

• • • • • • • • • • • • • • • •

LINE REMINDER

How soon we forget! How long has that line been on that reel? And, what kind was it?

My solution is a piece of yellow waterproof plastic tape attached to the reel foot before putting the reel on the rod.

The date, line type, and pound test are marked with a Sharpie® Permanent Marker with a fine point tip.

I try to replace the line on my reels every year, more frequently if it has been in heavy use.

FISHING REEL MAINTENANCE

If you want your fishing reels to last and perform well, constant attention and maintenance will help. A visual inspection after every trip might be a pain, but it can pay off in the long run.

Make sure that line rollers on spinning reels really roll. If they don't roll, the line will cut a groove in the roller and weaken the line. Line should fill the spool within 1/8" or so for best casting performance. Bail-return springs should be replaced if they don't close the bail smartly. Reel manufacturers recommend that drags be loosened between trips. Not many of us do that, but drags should be loosened in the off season on all reels. If the rod tip bounces up and down as line is pulled off the reel, this means the drag is jerky and could break the line and the drag washers need maintenance.

All reels should be cleaned and relubed at least once a year, preferably in the off season. If you don't have an off season, pick your own schedule and stick to it. Reels that get hard, everyday use, should get more frequent maintenance. Most reels can be cleaned and relubed by the average angler. However, I would leave maintenance of offshore lever drag reels to the manufacturer or a reliable tackle shop. These reels are far too complex for an average shade-tree mechanic like me to disassemble, etc.

Tools needed: Screwdrivers (use screwdrivers with non-tapered blades on high quality reels because a tapered blade can tear up a screw slot), assorted nut drivers or a 1/4-inch drive socket set, a small tin can with kerosene to clean off the old grease (no open flames nearby), an old toothbrush (not to be reused on teeth), plenty of old newspapers spread liberally around to absorb the mess, fresh new grease, and one or more paper egg cartons (paper cartons rather than the foam plastic cartons absorb the excess kero better) to hold parts sequentially as the reel is disassembled. It also helps to have the reel parts list and diagram handy in case your memory fails and you suddenly have questions about how all those parts relate to each other. You can also take a Polaroid® or use a camcorder to record the disassembly sequence.

I disassemble a reel with regular screwdrivers, but I make sure not to use undersized ones that chew up the screw slots. As each part is removed from the reel, I put it in the can of **kerosene** and scrub it with the toothbrush to remove dirt and old grease.

⚠ **Please do not use gasoline for cleaning reel parts—it is too dangerous!** I've had friends seriously burned when gasoline ignited from flames or a spark. Kerosene is also flammable, and care must be taken in using it, too.

When cleaned, each part goes into a separate sequentially-numbered depression in the egg carton. Drag washers are cleaned and restacked in the order they came off their axle or spindle for reassembly. Broken or badly worn parts should be replaced at this point.

Setup for disassembling a fishing reel for cleaning & maintenance.

On some of my old spinning reels, alternate drag washers were made of leather and steel or brass. If the leather was badly compressed or worn, I cut a new washer out of an old leather wallet. On a 1950s Luxor spinning reel I found that the complete drag range from "off" to "pop the line" was only about half a turn of the adjusting knob when I experimented with hard drag materials.

Before reassembling a reel, I regrease drag washers and gears and return them to the reel exactly in the reverse order from the way in which I removed them. I have tried several different types of grease on drag washers. Never Seez® high temperature grease seems to work well, but it needs to be replaced every year or it will thicken. Teflon® lubricants work well for some anglers. The green waterproof Drydene® grease I use on boat trailer bearings seems to work as well as any.

Outdoor writer Tom Goodspeed recommends using a dab of STP®. One can never go wrong with the reel manufacturer's own brand of lubricant. Take your choice, but you'll soon realize a clean, dependable well-lubricated reel makes for a more pleasurable fishing trip.

Once all of your reels are in good shape, you can keep them that way with frequent inspections and a freshwater rinse after each trip. Then let them dry out if you store them in an enclosed place. My reels are stored on their rods and hung on the garage ceiling, so they are dry before mildew or corrosion can damage them.

Some anglers spray their reels with WD40® or a similar product to protect it, but these include petroleum-based distillates which might damage fishing line.

REEL-FILLER SPOOL TENSION CLUTCH

Two small pieces of old floor carpet, one on either side of a reel filler spool, make a simple adjustable clutch so new line can be applied to reels under tension.

Cut two 4-inch squares of old carpet and punch a hole with an awl through the center of each piece. Carpeting with a short nap seems to work best, but shag and berber also work. Then, thread one piece of carpet on a screwdriver or an awl with the backing

side toward the awl handle, then thread on the line filler spool, and last the other piece of carpet with the nap side toward the spool.

Place the pointed end of the awl in a shop vise and adjust it so the friction on the spool puts slight tension on the line being wound onto the fishing reel, as shown in the photo above.

Next, thread the new line through the rod guides. Spinning reel bails should be open when the line is tied to the spool. Line on levelwind reels is threaded through the line leveling guide, tied to the spool axle, then the knot is pulled tight

After winding a small amount of line on a spinning reel against light tension, then stop and drop the rod tip a foot or so. If the slack line twists into a tight coil, turn the supply spool of line over, and wind more line on. Check again for line twist.

Line twist is the bane of all spinning reel anglers. Your first cast with twisted line will result in a gob of tangled line coming off the spool and wrapping around the rod guides. Properly installing line on the reel can solve that problem.

• • • • • • • • • • • • • • • • •

REEL PROTECTORS

Reels, sunglasses, and other items carried on fishing boats are likely to get scratched if not protected. I save old (clean) socks for that purpose.

Women's "footies" (really short fluffy socks) make nice reel covers. A regular sock will protect sunglasses or other items.

FISHING REEL LINE REMOVAL

The simplest way to remove old fishing line from a fishing reel is with a small hand-held electric drill.

First, a piece of scrap wood about the size of a pencil is tightened in the drill's chuck. Then, I secure the rod with the reel on it in a vise with a thick rag to protect the handle—or simply have someone hold the rod.

Next, the end of the line to be removed is tied to the stick. Revolving spool reels are placed in "free spool." For spinning reels remove line from the end of the spool. Run the drill until almost all of the line is off the spool, then go slowly to the end to prevent damage.

After cutting the old line at the reel spool, simply "unchuck" the piece of scrap wood and ball of old line and dispose of it. Some tackle shops have a recycling bin for old line.

Line is one of the least expensive items we use, and it is the weakest link between us and a possible record fish. Experts tell us it should be replaced frequently with new, fresh line.

This system can be used with all types and sizes of reels. It will save you time. The time you save is better spent fishing.

REEL TIPS

- Reversing the line on your reel can make the line last longer before you have to replace it. With the outside in, and vice versa, the unused inside portion will be practically like new. To get the line off the reel, I simply tie the outer end of the line to a tree and walk around the yard until all the line is off the reel. Then I cut the arbor knot that attaches the line to the reel spool. As I walk, I slide the line through my fingers to detect nicks or wear. My route takes me around trees to get the longest path, but not through any exposed dirt that the line could later transfer to the reel.

Next, I walk back to my starting point and untie the line from the tree and tie it to the reel spool. I wind the line back on the spool through my fingers again to provide some tension and remove any dirt or debris.

- One of the simplest ways to keep line on a spinning reel spool from unraveling is to tie a knot in a rubber band and slip it over the line on the spool. The knot becomes a "handle" to remove the rubber band.

- Trolling rotating lures like spoons and in-line spinners often twists fishing line. To remove the twist let the line out behind a moving boat with no terminal tackle attached—not even a snap swivel. Then reel in the line. Dragging the line through the water provides enough tension to untwist the line.

- Some anglers claim they get longer casts with a spinning reel if they rub a bit of car wax on the lip of the reel spool.

- Would you believe there is a simple fix for backlashes? Place your thumb (use two or three fingers for wider reels) on the spool and wind a couple of revolutions. Then, put the reel in "free spool" and pull the backlash out. I've tried it lots of times—it works most of the time.

- Sometimes monofilament fishing line has been stored in tackle shops or your tackle box too long. If your line has a dull, powdery look, it's probably out of date and has started to decompose. It has reduced strength and will break easier in this condition. When the new "superlines" begin to fray, replace them or reverse them, too.

• Insect repellent can play havoc with the finish on fly lines (as well as that of many other plastic articles) so rinse any bug juice off your hands thoroughly before handling fishing equipment.

• Superlines are so "slippery" they will often slide around the spool if not properly anchored to it. If you keep tightening your drag and you are able to pull out line anyway, check to see if the spool is rotating. If the spool is not rotating, remove the superline (I walked mine off around the yard), and put several yards of monofilament on the spool first, anchored with an arbor knot. Then tie the other end of the mono to the end of your superline with a blood knot, then wind it on the reel. If you had the reel spool filled to the brim originally, you may have to cut a few yards off the end of the line to offset the mono you installed.

• Superline often requires monofilament leaders to fool the fish. In a reverse situation, several Florida anglers use mono line on their reels, and superline as a toothy-critter leader.

• Fly anglers in search of record fish often need more backing on their new, large arbor reels. Some have replaced their dacron backing with braided superline which is much smaller in diameter per line test, and allows more backing. The trick to installing superlines on any reel is to put it on under pressure making sure to weave it back and forth as it goes on the reel. You want it to overlap in a crosswise fashion or it will bury in the underlying wraps and possibly break off a fish, bust a rod, or tear off a rod guide or two. Dacron stretches about 13 percent, braided superline stretches less than 4 percent, so fish might need to be played with a bit more finesse when using superline for backing.

• Superlines are so thin for their strength, and so slippery, that anglers who try to pull on the line to dislodge a plug stuck in or around structure can cut themselves right to the bone! Bass fishermen wrap the line several times around a 6- to 8-inch length of dowel for extra leverage and safety.

• It is also possible to break your fishing rod since the superlines are not as forgiving as monofilament. Set the hook gently!

The "Cannon Ball" Lure

LURE MODIFICATIONS

Innovative anglers often enjoy making or modify their baits, always looking for the "Ultimate Lure" that will make the difference between a full stringer and a busted trip. Some modify lures for other reasons: The pure satisfaction of catching a fish on something you made; something to do in the winter; replacing dangerous treble hooks with single ones; or simply removing treble hooks to make it easier to release fish so you won't have so many to clean or give away.

Sharp readers will ask: "If single hooks are so great, why don't the manufacturers rig every lure that way?" Good question. The answer, according to a Pradco representative (makers of Heddon, Cotton Cordell, Rebel, etc.) is that single hook plugs don't sell. Tests of sales from side-by-side displays of treble hook plugs next to the same lures with single hooks were interesting: All of the treble hook plugs sold out but no single hook lures moved. Buyers equate the number of hooks with numbers of fish caught. But, don't feel guilty if you buck the multiple treble hook trend— single hook lures account for plenty of fish.

It's a lot of fun to modify or make your own lures. And it's a real thrill to see a fish bite on some crazy contraption that was born in your own fevered brain. There is no lure too silly to show to a fish. I know—do it all the time.

Take Bill Cannon of Cambridge MD—his well-decorated 1-oz. sassy shad lure is shown on the opposite page. Bill wanted to cover all the bases in one superb lure for weakfish. In some areas like Delaware Bay, weakfish like purple worms. Bill added one. Stinger hooks often spell the difference between a hooked fish and a lost one. He added one with yellow feathers. A large whole shrimp topped off the conglomeration, which, in deference to his last name, I dubbed the "Cannon Ball." We caught weakfish up to 14 pounds on this lure combo, so don't make fun of it.

If necessity is the Mother of Invention, and imagination the Father, then it follows that innovation is the offspring. Let's take a look at some lures these parents bred in my home workshop.

Modified Lures Numbers 1 through 9

In the photo above **1/2-oz. Rat-L-Traps #1, #2, & #3** have been modified, with varying success. The top **Trap #1** carries a single jig-hook with the barb mashed down instead of two trebles. A jig-hook was used so it would ride upright and not snag things and a 4-inch swimmertail grub decorates the hook. The lure's nose digs down when retrieved, so the lure rides at a 45-degree angle with the grub swimming behind. Does it catch fish? Well, during the past striped bass season, this lure caught stripers on certain days. Other days, fish would slam it hard and not get hooked.

If you've ever cleaned a striper that had alewives stacked head-to-tail like sardines in its stomach, you'll know that fish sometimes hit lures head first, sometimes tail first. With two trebles I might have hooked every fish, but with meager bag limits, who needs to catch every fish? Also, the single barbless hook made it easy to release undersized fish. Largemouth bass in my pond snagged this lure every cast, suggesting they didn't decide to grab it until it rattled through their living room, then they had to catch it from behind.

Rat-L-Traps® **#2 and #3** have spinner blades in place of their belly or tail treble hooks. Largemouth bass and stripers liked both of these combinations, with the belly treble rig catching better, but a single tail treble more weed-free. I used a #12 snap swivel to attach the blades, trying both French and willow spinner blades with equal success.

Lure #4 is a 1/8-oz. Tiny Trap® and **lure #5 is a 1/5-oz. Storm Pee Wee Wart**®—both with their belly treble hooks removed. These tiny lures are deadly on white perch in the shallows in midsummer. The Wart wiggles a little deeper, but the perch will come up two feet to grab a Tiny Trap. An active 11-inch white perch can sink a tiny treble in your finger in a heartbeat, so that's why I remove the belly treble. The scars are gone now, but the memory remains. I tried a single #4 jig-hook instead of the tail treble, but missed too many strikes.

For those who like to mold their own bucktail jigs, **#6** and **#7 are 5/16-oz. Pony Head jigs** cast in a Do-It Mold. A 2/0 #635 jig-hook was used. Instead of using a #12 barrel swivel for the spinner blade, I substituted a Netcraft #61 bead chain cut in two pieces of different lengths, one for each lure. A split ring at the end of the bead chain allows attachment of a French or willow leaf blade. They were decorated with a 6" white or chartreuse swimmertail worm. Some makers paint their jigheads, some don't. The fish don't seem to mind either way. A tow test in the bathtub will help the experimenter decide on bead chain length and blade preference. I liked 7 beads and a willow leaf. Did it catch fish? No and yes. Pond bass ignored it, but Chesapeake Bay striped bass seemed very happy to see it.

Surface popping plugs #8 and #9 are just as productive as those with two treble hooks, but make it easier to release fish, particularly if you file or mash down the hook barb. Remember, though, if you remove the belly treble hook on a surface popper, you have to substitute a small piece of lead ballast in the belly to make the plug ride upright. The **white Herter's popper #8** has a small slug of lead in its belly hole. **Lure #9 is a factory-made Z-faced Atom Popper** that comes with a belly weight. A small piece of bucktail at the tail helps face this lure toward the angler for a better "pop."

Modified Lures Numbers 10 through 15

There are lots of things to do with spinner and buzz blades. The saltwater-size **spinnerbait** #10 in the above photo, was cast in a modified Herter's "Popeye" jig mold. (Herter's once sold fishing lures). Heavy wire (.045") was necessary for this Godzilla-strength spinnerbait. A French spinner blade and bucktail hair complete the rig. This is a great striper lure in summer or early fall before the first cold snap when the water clears. In clear water, stripers seem wire shy.

Baits #11 and #12 are similar to weighted walleye spinner lures. This is basically a good idea to combine sinker, spinner blade, and hook in one lure, but it is not popular everywhere. They were cast in old Herter's molds, using .045" wire in place of hooks. Then a clevis, spinner blade, and beads were added to the tail shaft before a loop to hold the hook was formed. Live or cut bait can be added to the hook, or a 4" plastic grub in the color of your choice. Having the line attachment point on top of the weighted head is an advantage. The lure rides upright and keeps the spinner blade from twisting the line. These lures are better for casting. Trolling them would twist the line anyway. More about line twist later.

The top right **buzz bait #13** slid nicely over lily pads in a bass river. We could see bass charging through the lily pads behind it, and when it reached open water, Bingo! This one is easy to make with .035" wire, a buzz bait propeller, the grommet from a pop rivet, a bullet worm weight, and hook of your choice. Mine is decorated with a 7-1/2" Culprit pearl worm.

The bottom two conglomerations on the right are interesting: One is a great fish-getter, the other twists line before it hits the water. **Lure #14** was molded with .035" wire in place of the hook in a 1/2-oz. ruby lips jig mold. Then a buzz bait propeller was added with a bead behind it. A long shank hook accommodates a 7-1/2" Culprit worm. Unfortunately on the first cast everything wrapped around the main line. A short piece of stiff wire leader solved that problem. This lure makes so much commotion and looks so silly underwater that when I caught stripers on it I was probably more surprised than the fish.

Lure #15, while easily made from .035"wire, a bullet weight, a buzz bait propeller, a bead, and a hook—was a flop. It twisted line badly because the attachment point is in a direct line with the propeller shaft. I included this *flopperoo* as a bad example to show the reader that every modification isn't successful.

But, I'll keep trying until I make the "Ultimate Lure."

If one of your "Ultimate Lures" looks so good in the water you want to jump right in after it, stop right there. You've got a winner!

MAKE YOUR OWN PLUGS

"Holy cow!" Jack Stovall hollered, "Did you see that strike?" A big striper had grabbed Stovall's homemade copy of a famous bottleneck popper and wrapped it around a tree trunk quicker than it takes to tell about it. Either the tree or the fish now owned the lure. I groaned. Stovall's beautiful, lathe-turned, airbrush-painted plugs are a work of art. The one he gave me is in a trophy case, untouched. It's too pretty to fish.

Stovall tied on another handcrafted masterpiece. "I've gotta see that again," he said. It was a slow-motion replay of the same act. One pop next to the fallen tree and Ka-plooey! The plug disappeared in the midst of a huge splash and a swirl the size of a bath tub. Our craftsman-angler sighed and tied on another shiny new plug. Next, a third replay, but in fast-forward. Somebody down there now owned three magnificently-painted wooden works of art.

I saw Stovall rooting around in his tackle box.

"What are you looking for?" I asked.

"Something cheaper," he replied.

Three minutes, three lures lost—plugs that probably took at least three hours each to make. Was it worth it? You bet. The memory of those strikes will long out last the pain of lure loss. And you can bet Stovall is spending time the next long, cold winter making more lures to toss at that same log next May.

Some angler-craftsmen, like Stovall, can look at a lure, or even a picture in a tackle catalog, then go back to their shop and make a copy. And have a lot of fun doing it, too. They might make some changes in body style, paint the bait differently, or not paint it at all in the case of lead jigheads or spinner baits.

Stovall started making lures because he couldn't find modern wood versions of his favorites: Heddon's Lucky 13 and Vamp-Spook. Those and other oldies like the Creek Chub Darter were too valuable as "antiques" to toss at fish. Once, he made a Boone Castana look-alike because an original couldn't be found in the catalogs. Someone who had a Castana said it was a hot snook and speckled trout bait in Florida, where Stovall was headed on vacation. Was his version a great lure? You bet.

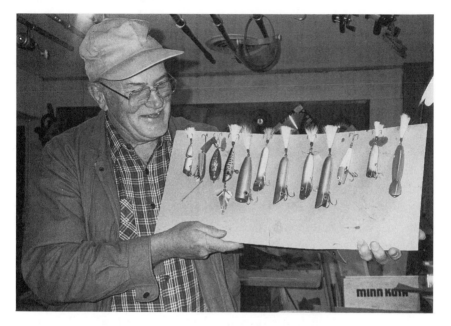

Jack Stovall with a display of his homemade plugs.

While a wood lathe allows more flexibility in the design, good lures can be made from broom, shovel, or rake handles. Closet rod is another quick way to get a round piece of wood. A simple popper can be made by scooping out a concave nose and rounding off the tail.

"I like seasoned white cedar for its lightness," Stovall said recently. "Sometimes, dowel woods are too heavy—they won't float. Closet rod is OK if it's light enough." Stovall has a small wood lathe, so making lathe-turned lures is not a problem. He uses a Dremel tool to hollow out a concave face for poppers. After shaping the body, he sands it on the lathe. Before painting, the plug gets three coats of auto paint primer. Some lures get a Rustoleum primer, with sanding between coats.

He always checks out his floaters in a tub of water before painting. For small fish lures, he uses small screw eyes for hook hangers. Larger lures including those for big stripers, get brass sinker eyes for hook hangers, epoxied into drilled holes in the plug. He doesn't like split rings, so he makes open-eye hooks by cutting the eye of a treble with heavy duty diagonal pliers.

⚠ If you try this, make sure you are wearing eye protection to avoid bits of metal flying off the hooks! He attaches the hooks after the painting is finished.

Hooks can be held in place with screw eyes unless big stripers and blues are expected. Drilling through the length of the plug so it can be through-wired gives the big-fish angler a feeling of security. The popper's tail hook can be decorated with bucktail hair to act as a rudder that keeps the lure aimed at the angler after each "pop."

Painting lures has become an art form to Stovall. He paints his lures with an air brush! Then he adds stick-on eyes, and the lure gets a last coat of clear varnish. His lures have already been weighted for proper balance. Stovall's baits have a dark topside, silver sides, and the bottoms are painted orange, yellow, or white. The cup on a popper's face is usually red.

Painting the lure gives the craftsman a sense of pride, but fish are looking up at the bait's bottom. They see the plug in silhouette, and must quickly decide if it looks like lunch.

For the average angler just starting out to make his own plugs, it might be smart to buy some unpainted wood or plastic plug bodies from Netcraft, Cabela's, or other tackle supplier. Finish them by painting and hanging hooks. Then decide whether to pursue the hobby of making them from scratch.

For those who want to go a step further I suggest getting a copy of C. Boyd Pfeiffer's book "Modern Tackle Craft" which goes into much more detail than can be included here. See the Bibliography.

However, if one decides to make wood plugs from scratch, a band or jig saw is necessary to cut out the blanks, and some shop tools like a saw, wood rasp, sander, and drill should be at hand.

Larger saltwater plugs are through-wired for strength, so a long electrician's drill is necessary.

Painting can be as elaborate as Stovall's airbrush decorating, or as simple as two coats of enamel with a small brush.

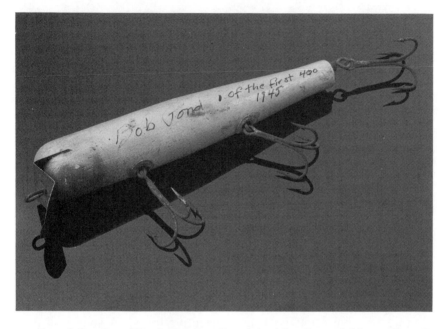

One of the first 400 of Bob Pond's original handcarved "Atom Plugs."

You never know when you'll come up with a hot lure design, so it pays to experiment. It's not only fun during the winter doldrums, but the right lure could provide you with extra income.

Fifty years ago, Cape Cod striper angler Bob Pond turned out 400 wooden swimming plugs, essentially super-large Creek Chub swimmer look-alikes. Stripers loved them. Geyser-like eruptions under Pond's plugs reminded WWII-era anglers of the atom bomb explosions then in the news, so he called his lure the "Atom Plug." That lure and others he designed provided Bob with a living for 50 years—plus some of the best fishing imaginable.

We should all be so lucky!

MAKING BULLETPROOF BUCKTAILS

Bucktail jig-making is another way to cure the winter blahs. No one ever has enough of these effective lures. A source of lead and a well-ventilated place to melt the metal are necessary, plus a jig mold, hooks, scissors, heavy leather gloves, thread and a bobbin, and a natural white or color-dyed bucktail.

Follow the mold maker's directions to make the leadheads, then let them cool. Years ago, I painted the heads with leftover white or yellow rust-proofing enamel. It chipped badly. One good smack against a concrete bridge piling, and the paint was gone. Next I tried vinyl paints; the jigs were pretty and durable, but the paint fumes were unpleasant.

Lately, I've used powder paint with great success. Properly cured, this heat-setting epoxy powder is nearly bulletproof. I have dented the lead under properly prepared powder paint, but the lure's finish didn't even chip! First, hold the jig by the hook with a pair of pliers. Then, heat the leadhead with a heat gun until the lead is very warm to the touch. After stirring the powder paint to loosen it, dip the heated jighead into the powder, quickly remove it, and tap the hook on the container to dislodge excess powder. You can watch the paint turn to a nice glossy finish. If the finish is dull, heat it until it glosses. If the finish bubbled, the metal was too hot. Toss it away, or at bluefish.

Hang your painted jig to cool. One coat of powder paint is durable enough for average use. But, if you go one extra step, the finish is almost chip-proof. Hang the jig in the oven and bake it for 15 minutes at 300 degrees, then let it cool again.

Ron Adamecz of Annapolis, MD hangs six or eight bucktail jigheads on the rim of a tin can and heats them in a toaster oven at 325 degrees F, his ideal temperature for the black powder paint he favors. He modified the rack in his toaster oven with four bolts to accommodate the tin can's height. After removing the jigheads individually with a pair of pliers and dipping them in the powder paint, he hangs them to cool. When they are all cool he puts them back on the tin can and bakes them in the toaster oven at 300 degrees F for 10 minutes, then lets them cool with the oven off and its door open. Clay Gooch of St. Michaels, MD also uses a toaster oven to heat several jigheads at a time, but he simply hangs his on the oven rack.

After the lead is cool, tie on the bucktail hair, lock the thread in place with a dab of super glue, and go fishing. For additional durability, I usually skip the super glue and slip a 3/4-inch long piece of 1/2-inch diameter electrician's heatshrink tubing over the jighead to cover the thread. Then I cover the bucktail hair with a piece of aluminum foil to prevent singing and use the heat gun to shrink the tubing and lock the threads in place. One commercial jig maker wraps chemical-shrink tape over the thread. The resulting bucktail jig not only looks nice, but will outlast the average jig many times.

I have caught (and released) over 200 stripers on one of my "bulletproof bucktails" and it still has all its hair and paint, though the shrink tubing has been roughened by many striper gums. One of my jigs has been in use for three striper seasons!

This shows the progression: Heatshrink tubing - tied bucktail - bucktail with tubing slipped over the thread - bucktail with tubing heated & shrunk.

Once the midwinter lure craftsman gets in the swing of it with jig molds, hooks, wire, beads, and other goodies, experimenting with other lures like spinnerbaits comes naturally. Molding a 1-oz. jighead on a .047" wire spinnerbait form was a successful experiment for me. Basically a heavy duty bass-style spinnerbait with bucktail hair dressing the head, my lure cast nicely on heavy spinning gear and caught a lot of shallow-water stripers.

Bass anglers can buy a spinnerbait mold and preformed wires to cut their labor. Spinnerbait heads and blades can be decorated with the previously-mentioned powder paint; some lure makers even use an ear syringe to blow a contrasting shade of powder paint on the background color before it cools. Very artistic! ⚠ Don't use the ear syringe in your ear after it has held powder paint!

Other accessories include all kinds of brass-and-glass noisemakers or clackers, high quality ball bearing swivels, and metal blades. Many of these designs are attractive to bass, but anglers must please themselves first, before showing their creations to lower forms of marine life.

JIG POURING TIPS

- When pouring lead jigs and sinkers make sure you have good ventilation. Use heavy gloves and wear eye protection.
- Use soft lead for jigs. Melted wheel weights often don't fill out the cavity of a jig mold very well, but can be used for sinkers.
- Good molds are worth their price. Cheap molds leave a lot of flash that has to be trimmed off. They also make lumpy jigs which will give your friends a good laugh.
- "Smoke" the mold with a candle flame before using. Carbon helps release jigs from the mold easier.
- Heat the mold before adding hooks by pouring several jigheads without hooks. Save the resulting ingots for remelting.
- Hooks must fit the mold neatly for best results. Overlarge hooks can keep the mold from closing all the way.
- Some people give the jigheads one coat of paint before tying on bucktail hair. When the hair is tied on, another coat of paint seals the thread. This does not apply to powder paint.

Bob Meushaw with his famous feather jigs.

- Custom-machined precision molds like the one made years ago for Bob Meushaw's famous Chesapeake Bay feather jigs might fit together so tightly air can't escape. That doesn't allow the lead to fill out the mold. Bob's machinist scribed several lines across the mold's open faces to let trapped air out.

• Fine wire jig-hooks give better penetration and bend easily when caught in a log or sometimes in a fish. Tinned jig-hooks with an O'Shaughnessy bend are better suited to saltwater applications and big fish.

• Jig molds can be modified. Chuck Prahl's modified spinnerbait mold (above) makes a great spearpoint bucktail jig that has become a very popular striped bass lure. Chuck used a Dremel tool with a round stone to make the concave recess in the mold for the #635T eye jig-hook he wanted to use. The small channel where the spinnerbait wire went was left alone—it leaves a small amount of flash that can easily be trimmed.

SALTWATER-SIZE THREAD BOBBINS

Saltwater anglers who tie their own bucktail jigs can easily make a heavy-duty thread bobbin from lamp parts to accommodate heavy "E" size thread on 100-yard or larger spools. The bobbin can be customized to individual lure maker's needs.

To make each of my two bobbins, I used the following parts: one piece of 3/8" all-thread lamp pipe in the proper length, two 3/8" lamp pipe nuts, one 3/8" pull chain switch bushing, and a piece of perforated car radio support strap 3/4 wide x 1/16 thick x 6 in. long, (from an old car radio installation), and a 1/4"-20 x 2-1/2" long bolt and 1/4"-20 lock nut.

First, bend the radio support strap in a vise into a "U" shape to accommodate your spool of thread. Then, drill a 13/32" or 7/16" hole in the center of the "U" to fit the 3/8" lamp pipe.

⚠ Tighten the strap in a vise while drilling for safety reasons.

I used a 2" piece of lamp pipe on one bobbin, and a 3" piece on the other one to allow enough clearance to wrap thread on bucktail jigs with small or large heads. First, remove any sharp edges on the lamp pipe or bushing that will cut or abrade your thread. Secure the lamp pipe to the "U" shaped strap with two 3/8" lamp nuts. Screw the 3/8" pull chain switch bushing on the other end of the lamp pipe. Place the 100-yard spool of thread in the "U" and secure it with the 1/4" bolt and nut. Adjust spool tension by tightening the lock nut.

A 14" piece of stiff leader wire bent double makes a good bobbin threader. Lamp parts are available from lamp or hardware stores. Radio support straps are available from car radio installers.

An "emergency" thread bobbin for tying hair on bucktail jigheads can be made from a short length of 1/8" or so diameter aluminum or copper ground wire. Make a circle bend on each end of the wire to accommodate the 1/4" bolt and Nylock nut. Then bend a larger circle at the midpoint in the wire to make the thread captive. Tighten the nut so the thread bobbin does not drop.

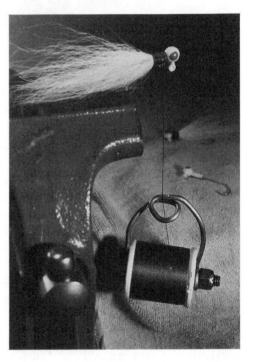

In use, thread is pulled off the bobbin for a foot or so at a time, and the thread is wound onto the jighead by directing it through your fingers.

RUBBER CEMENT AIDS BUCKTAIL TYING

Controlling a loose hank of bucktail hair while making those first few thread wraps to hold it in place on a jighead can be really frustrating for novice and even some expert tiers.

Atom Lure manufacturer, Bob Pond, passed on a tip that has been a big help to uncoordinated home-tiers like me.

First, drop a glob of rubber cement on a plastic lid. Cut a hank of hair off the deer tail and swish the cut end around in the rubber cement. Place several cemented hanks around the lid to dry as shown in the above photo. Then, with a jighead in the vise, scissor the cemented end of a clump of hair off squarely. Spread the hair evenly around the jig and secure it with thread. You'll find it stays in place and there are no loose hairs to fall out. Finish-wrap and super-glue the thread, or cover it with heatshrink tubing. See page 143.

You can even work in a breezy area with rubber-cemented bucktail hair. It won't blow around like loose hair. A dab of rubber cement can eliminate the frustration factor and speed up bucktail jig-tying for novice and pro alike.

MAKING MINI-SPINNERBAITS

White perch and white bass are favorites on the table. They are both close cousins of the striped bass, and are worthy opponents on ultralight spinning gear and mini-spinnerbaits. You can buy a store-bought version for a dollar or so, but once you get the jig mold, lead, hooks, wire, round-nose pliers, ball-bearing swivels, and spinner blades, you can make hundreds of these perch-getters for nearly the same unit cost. The difference is in the fun of making your own successful lures.

To make mini-spinnerbaits, I first cast about 100 1/8-oz. and 1/16-oz. jigheads on #4 and #6 jig-hooks. Paint them if it makes you happy, but perch and whites don't care. Next, buy or bend up some wire forms from .024" to .027" wire, copying a store-bought model. Attach a tiny jig to one end of the V-shaped wire form and a #12 snap swivel to the opposite arm of the wire. Add a #1 chrome French spinner blade (my favorite) or a #3 chrome Swiss Swing blade to the snap swivel. Next, add a 2" white (or your favorite color) plastic grub to the jig-hook, and you're ready to fish.

A 'POXY ON YOUR FLY

Coastal fishing guides and tackle shops have noticed an ever-expanding interest in saltwater fly-fishing in recent years. Modern saltwater fly tackle and synthetic fly-tying materials have allowed briny anglers to go after bigger, toothier game fish than flimsier freshwater fly gear would tolerate. Durable synthetics like crimped nylon have replaced polar bear and bucktail hair in many saltwater fly patterns. In addition, flies made of 5-minute epoxy are nearly indestructible, no matter how sharp a critter's dentures. Called Mother Of Epoxy, or MOE, these early flies have spawned the ever-increasing variety of artsy and colorful flies one sees now.

Clockwise from top left: Epoxy Silverside, Mylar Sand Eel, Stealth Fly, and Glass Minnow—all by D. L. Goddard of Easton, MD.

Bob Popovics of Seaside Park, NJ is one of the Mid-Atlantic area's best known MOE fly innovators. In 1974, his first MOE flies were "crude," he said, and made of polar bear and bucktail hair. Bluefish rapidly destroyed them. He tied some MOEs with

Ultra Hair and hair loss decreased. Surf and bay anglers soon found Popovics' epoxy-bodied flies were so tough you couldn't wear them out.

Both epoxy and silicone adhere well to fly-tying materials. Good. Both products also stick to hands, clothes, and tools with a terrible tenacity. Bad.

Lefty Kreh wets his hands in a cup of water containing 6 to 8 drops of dishwasher Jet-Dry® to keep them from sticking while shaping both 5-minute epoxy and silicone flies. Lefty now uses clear silicone caulk for fly bodies. "It's flexible, clear, and you can mold it with your fingertips as it starts to dry," Kreh said, "silicone lets the feathers or hair work better than a hard epoxy body does. Also, fish might be more likely to hang onto a body of soft silicone. Sink rates are about the same for both epoxy and silicone-bodied flies."

MOEs can be balanced with lead wire, BB shot, or lead eyes placed opposite the hook point to make the fly ride hook up. Doll eyes opposite the point of the hook make the fly ride hook down. Stiff mono can be tied in before epoxying as a weed guard.

Beach or boat, epoxy-head streamer or MOE fly, anyway you do it, be advised that saltwater fly-fishing is coming on fast.

Build some MOE flies and dunk them in the salt when big stripers or blues are around. You're in for a thrill.

LURE TIPS

• Many lure and rig-making accessories can be found in craft stores. Doll eyes, beads, yarn, glitter, and many other goodies can be found there. Let your imagination run wild.

• Hit flea markets and garage sales for trinkets to add to, or make, lures. Old earrings can be added to spinnerbaits for extra pizazz.

• Other homey items for lure making include kitchenware. Some anglers haunt flea markets and garage sales looking for knives and spoons to make casting lures, the fancier the better for extra glitter. I made a deep-jigging spoon from an old stainless steel table knife, but it was impossibly hard to cut with a saw. I had to grind the blade off. Drilling a hole in each end of the handle for a large split ring allows for a hook at one end and the fishing line at the other. The bowl of a tablespoon makes a good wobbler, again by drilling two holes and adding a hook. Save the spoon handle to make yet another lure. Bend the handles for more action. Slap on a little paint and/or some large eyes. Try out their action in the bathtub or a local pond and make adjustments if necessary. These make great deep-jigging spoons in fresh or saltwater.

• Add glitter and neon-enhanced fabric paints to all manner of lures including crankbaits, poppers, and plastics to attract fish.

• Red and black waterproof Sharpie® permanent marker pens can be used to enhance the appearance of bucktail jigs. Use the black Sharpie to make stripes across the bucktail hair in a raccoon-tail pattern, and the red marker to make a red "gill" on the head. Some anglers believe these enhancements help them catch more fish.

• Carry a bottle or two of quick-drying nail polish in the boat. You may want to change the color of a lure on short notice. Anglers who use small jigheads coated with powder paint carry 35-mm plastic film cans of the material in different colors on their boats for the same reason. They warm the jighead with a cigarette lighter, dip it in the powder and make a cast.

• The eyes have it. Game fish chasing baitfish are said to *key* on the eyes. Add eyes, the larger the better, to jigheads, plugs, worm weights, and offshore trolling lures. Dab a common nail (with a head) in bright color paint to place the outer ring of an eye on your jighead, worm weight, or plug. After drying, dab a finishing nail (with no head) in black paint and make the center, or iris of the eye. Colored glue from the craft store can be used to make eyes. Get two different, contrasting colors and apply it to worms, tube baits, weights, etc. Boyd Pfeiffer glues a single doll eye on the underside of his fly rod poppers—"that's what the fish sees" he says. Painted eyes, doll eyes, and stick-ons, covered with clear epoxy or varnish, could increase your catch ratio, some experts say.

• Add a Rubbercore® or pinch-on sinker to the lower leg of a spinnerbait to make it run deeper.

• To add a rattle to a spinnerbait, slip a piece of heatshrink tubing over the hook and put a rattle in it before shrinking the tubing with heat. A small rattle can also be superglued to a large spinner blade or placed inside a plastic grub before putting on the hook.

• Drilling holes in the outer tips of buzzbait blades will disturb more water as you pull the bait along. Some anglers drill holes in spoons for the same reason.

⚠ **WARNING:** Always anchor a blade or spoon in a vise before drilling, because the drill bit can bind and spin the metal piece around like a knife blade.

• Tiny dentist's rubber bands (above), or snips of small-diameter tubing, can be used on "R-shaped" spinnerbait or buzz bait wires in case the angler uses snaps or snap swivels. This keeps the snap from migrating up one or the other wires and tangling the line.

• To use an old spinnerbait as a sinker, cut off the hook just behind the leadhead, remove the spinner blades, and attach a baited hook or short leader and lure instead. Attach the fishing line in the same place as you would normally.

• Cut the leadhead off an old buzz bait and bend a circle at the wire's end. Attach it to a floating Rat-L-Trap® or other shallow-running crankbait. Buzz it along in the shallows.

• Use a wooden coffee stirrer to make a slot, or use a drinking straw to hollow out a tunnel, in a plastic worm for a rattle or attractant. Fix the rattle in place with a dab of super glue.

• Save your old bloodworms, says Ted Sheridan of Mr. Wiffle® soft plastic lures. He squeezes out the "blood" and soaks his Mr. Wiffles in it. He takes spot, croaker, flounder, and sea bass with them. "I used one soaked bait all day," he said.

• Plastic worms can be repaired with a match or a hot needle by heating the broken ends and holding them together until they bond.

- Plastic bass worms can be fished efficiently by hooking them on a small ball jighead. If you want them to "float" higher in the water column on the retrieve in shallow water, use a flat (parallel to the bottom) jighead instead.

- Zippered plastic bags are great places to store plastic worms and grubs. Because they can bleed together store each color separately. I squush out the air and store the rolled bags in a clear #3700 Plano box.

- Jigheads can be rigged weedless in plastic tube baits. Simply hide the hook inside the tube.

- Screw a French blade to the bottom of a jighead like a crankbait lip to make it "swim."

- Another way to make jigheads, worms or grubs weedless is to make some small coils from leader wire (looks like a coil spring) and make a loop in one end of the coil. The loop hooks into the jig's eye (center lure in the photo below), and the grub or worm is threaded on the coil. Hide the hook point in the grub (far left in the photo).

- Use bread bag wire ties to keep the worm or grub from sliding down the hook (far right lure above) —or put a small dab of super glue gel on the hook shank before installing the plastic grub or worm.

• Stuff a rigged tube-jig with cotton, using a toothpick, says outdoor writer Bob Jones, and soak the cotton with your favorite oil-base fish attractant. Works in fresh or saltwater, he says. I found a piece of sponge works, too. The stuffed tube will often float if rigged without a leadhead jig.

• Tube lure "tentacles" can be made to flare out better by gluing a small, round piece of sponge to the hook inside the tube— soak it with attractant if you like.

• A soft tube or squid jig can be made almost weedless by threading a leader through the tube, sliding an egg sinker up the leader until it is inside the tube, then hiding the hook in the soft plastic.

• Some anglers put pieces of rock salt into a tube bait to attract bass bites.

• In similar fashion, says Captain George Fromm of Neavitt, MD, a piece of rubber or plastic tubing glued to the shank of a bucktail-jig's hook flares the hair out to make a more attractive bait. It can also hold a piece of pork rind farther up the hook shank.

• According to Storm Lures, two baits are better than one, as evidenced by their "Double Bug®," one Chug Bug® behind another. Almost any two lures can be connected by removing the tail hook on the lead lure and coupling the two tail-to-head with a split ring.

• In addition to the lure modifications discussed previously, some lures work just as well if fished backwards! Simply remove the tail hook and attach the line in its place. Then, split-ring the tail hook at the "front" of the plug. Bob Pond of Atom Lures® saw Cape Cod anglers doing that to his big swimming plugs. His "Reverse Atom" plug was a big hit in 1947 and is still selling!

• If you replace the treble hooks on a favorite plug with single hooks, be aware that the new hooks can change the balance of the lure. In some cases, you can clip off one tine of the treble to make a double hook without changing the plug's balance. If a large single hook replaces a treble, use a heavier split-ring to keep the plug on even keel.

• Weighting the tail of a popping or cigar-shaped surface plug makes it act like a dying baitfish when you stop its forward motion.

It should lie face up, tail down, in the water. A small hole drilled in the popper's bottom near the tail will accommodate a piece of super-glued lead solder. Several manufactured cigar-shaped topwater baits are weighted with a large steel bearing in a cavity near the lure's tail.

•   All manner of throwaway items can become fishing lures. Fountain pen bodies are made into poppers for striped bass and bluefish. A short piece of copper pipe can be sharpened at one end to be used to punch out foam plastic popper bodies. Tampon applicators (I'm not making this up) have been used to make bluefish lures in the long Island, NY area. They wash up on the beaches near sewer outfalls. A clean water group picked them up and made the lures as a fund-raiser.

•   Salty anglers have substituted single hooks for the trebles on diamond-shaped deep jigs for years. They cover the tail hooks with colored surgical tubing, which defies bluefish teeth. A smaller freshwater version can be made by substituting a single hook for the treble on a casting spoon and decorating it with a plastic worm or grub, rigged weedless.

•   Chesapeake Bay striper anglers have fished "dummy lines" ever since trolling was invented. This is meat-fishing, not at all sporty. A piece of clothes rope is tied to a cleat on the boat at one end and a sash weight (honest!) at the other, a sort of simple downrigger. Then a 50-pound test leader with a bucktail jig at the business end is tied to the sash weight. Old-time anglers tied in a screen door spring for a bit of stretch; recently, a "rubber snubber" does the same job. Huge stripers to 60-plus pounds, have been caught on these meat hooks.

•   A recent sportier spin-off on the dummy line idea can be trolled on a heavy outfit. Special hefty jig molds have been made to accommodate a 12/0 hook and heavy-duty line eye. The mold cavity holds two pounds of lead and is spear-shaped with a collar at the rear to tie on bucktail hair. The late Paul Vodak of Annapolis, MD told me it took the hair from an entire buck's tail to make one of these big-fish getters.

• The ever-popular parachute lures above, composed of crinkled chartreuse nylon strands tied on a bucktail jighead in the fashion of the offshore "seawitch," often gets a bit messy after use. George Bentz of Pasadena, MD says "Hold the head straight up and let the nylon hang down. Use a hairdryer to blow air on it, and the 'hair' will lay back as it would when towed through the water. Use a comb if necessary." He then wraps his much neater lure in aluminum foil to keep it that way.

• Bucktail and fly tiers can temporarily place a short section of plastic tubing over the barb and point of their hooks to keep the hook point from slicing their fingers every time the thread is wound around the hook.

• Chrome plated water pipe left over from plumbing your bathroom toilet makes a great lure for toothy critters like bluefish. Simply hammer each end of the pipe flat so you can drill holes for split rings to accommodate the line on one end and a hook on the other. Copper tubing has been used in the same way, and covered with highly reflective tape. Bend the pipe slightly for an enticing wiggle on the retrieve.

• Maryland outdoor writer Bill Burton bent a piece of flat iron several times to resemble a series of "steps." In the side view, it looked like a three-foot long piece of flat steel shaped like two letter "Ws" put together. He painted it white, drilled holes in one end for an 8/0 hook and another in the other end for the line attachment, and trolled it for striped bass. He made two legal catches with his "lure."

• Emergency lures or flies can be made from hooks decorated with pipe cleaners. Simply wind pipe cleaners in various colors or silver tinsel around a suitable hook as in the left photo.

• For extra zip, attach a spinner blade to the rear end of a lure, the fly described above, or an offshore trolling bait with a snap swivel by bending down the hook barb, slipping the snap swivel over it, and prying the barb back into position.

• Any number of materials can be attached to a hook and trolled with success. Chesapeake Bay anglers once added a strip of red flannel to a bucktail jig. Later, Uncle Josh® dyed pork rind strips, which have been popular for decades were added. Offshore anglers can make a strip bait from nylon strap webbing or kerosene heater wicks.

• Surgical tubing lures can be made in various lengths for coastal game fish. The tubing can be tinted in many colors with fabric dyes. Stiff stainless steel wire with a stainless steel hook at one end is threaded through the beveled end of the hose, and the opposite end is pulled back enough to attach the wire to a swivel at the "head" of the lure. The internal wire can be bent to make the lure "swim" when trolled.

• Fly tier D. L. Goddard of Easton, MD makes a reversible slider/popper by dressing a long shank hook with bucktail or feathers, then making a popper body with a tapered rear end from dense foam plastic. The eye of the hook is inserted through the lure from the rear toward the cupped face to make a popper, and through the popper face toward the rear to make a slider.

• The person who develops a smelly bait that closely resembles live baits like crab or shrimp will inherit the world, says lure inventor Greg Rhoten of Virginia. "Ever notice how fish ignore freshly-deceased crab?" he says. "And how they pounce on live baits?" Rhoten is convinced live baitfish and other prey emit a chemical that, when it is discovered and added to fishing lures, will forever change the word "fishing" to "catching."

• Lure storage gets to be a problem when the angler accumulates too many baits that absolutely will be used some day. I had small and large tackle boxes of every description scattered around the garage which held an assortment of goodies that had absolutely nothing to do with each other. The way I solved the problem was described in the Tackle Storage Lockers section on page 24.

• Offshore anglers have caught billfish with a rag mop-looking trolling lure with no hooks—it is simply a few strands of strong carpet yarn. Billfish wrap their bills around the "mop" and it entangles them. This is not considered "sport-fishing" by many IGFA anglers. But...

• I had the thought that the "hook and loop" principle might be transferred to a bass lure. Take off the hooks and cover a hard crankbait with the opposite of whatever lines the bass' mouth. If his dentures are hooky, cover the lure with loop material, or vice-versa. Seems to me if a bass took a bite, the hook and loop principle might hold the fish long enough to get him in the boat—and released without even a hook wound.

BASIC SALTWATER RIGS

This page is from the 1941 Edward vom Hofe Tackle Catalog.

MAKING RIGS

The saltwater rigs on the opposite page are as popular now as they were in 1941, when they appeared in the catalog of a long-out-of-business tackle company. They are basic, and they still work for bait-fishing in fresh or saltwater. (Notice the *1941* plea on the bottom of the page to make striped bass a game fish).

However, anglers are always trying to modify and/or improve upon the basics. The rigs on the following pages are a few that I have found helpful. You can make them effortlessly from materials in your tackle box, or from items easily obtained at your local tackle shop.

One bottom rig we find useful can be tied from a length of clear 30-pound test monofilament line in your shop or on the boat. We first called it the "Delaware Nothinball Rig," because that's where it originated, but since it has gained wide acceptance, we now call it the "do nothin' rig," or DNR for short. The difference in this rig is the hook is on the end of the rig, and the sinker is threaded on the next-to-the-end loop. We find it as good for bottom fishing with bait as any commercially-tied two-hook bottom rig, easy to make, and certainly a lot cheaper.

To make the DNR, cut a 48-inch length of 20- or 30-pound test monofilament line and tie a hook on one end (see drawing on the following page. I use 1/0 laser-sharpened Kahle hooks for seatrout, striped bass and croakers. Larger or smaller hooks for your specific quarry might make it necessary to increase or decrease line strength (and diameter). Next, slip a 1/4 x 3/4-inch rig float on the opposite end of the line and slide it next to the hook. Next, make a dropper loop about 12 inches from the hook. See the Knots chapter starting on page 179. This is for the sinker, so make the loop large enough to accommodate the sinker you plan to use. Then, tie another dropper loop about 12 inches from the last one. Make this loop stand out about 2 inches. Slip a spinner blade and a bead or two on this loop, then thread the loop through the eye of another 1/0 Kahle hook and drop the hook point through the loop to make it captive. The top end of the rig gets a perfection loop to connect to the snap swivel on the end of the fishing line.

A swivel could also be used as a connector between line and rig. Moisten all knots before tightening them. This rig gives you short leaders and, I feel, a quicker and more sensitive connection to a fish bite. The total length of the finished rig will be about 30 inches, but this is not critical. Fish don't care about precision.

DNR RIG

DROPPER LOOP

PERFECTION LOOP

DROPPER LOOP

SPINNER & BEADS

KAHLE 1/0 HOOK

SINKER ON A DROPPER LOOP

RIG FLOAT

KAHLE 1/0 HOOK

1.
2.
3.
4.

X

FLOUNDER RIGS

"Flounderologists" are always experimenting—some in the interest of science, others trying to find the perfect rig that flatfish just can't resist. Our flounder rig has been modified again and again in recent years. What began as a simple hook baited with a minnow has evolved into a three-foot piece of 20- or 30-pound test leader decorated with spinning blades, tied to a three-way swivel that allows for a short drop sinker. All sorts of attractors have found their way into our terminal tackle, and true believers think these shiny, noisy additions attract flounder.

*Jack Stovall's buzz blade flounder rig baited with
a silverside minnow and a strip of squid.*

Jack Stovall gets credit for adding a huge aluminum bass buzz bait blade in front of the hook. At Chincoteague, VA Stovall bailed one flounder after another while Mark Galasso and I patiently watched. Luckily, Stovall had some extra rigs, which Galasso and I later copied for our own use.

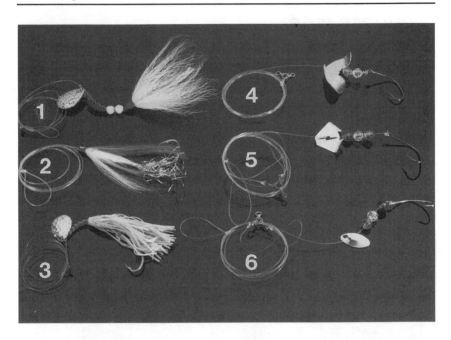

Conventional flounder rigs are shown in the left column in the above photo: **Rigs #1 and #2** designed to be dragged along the bottom, were tied by Captain Dick Arnold of Cape Charles, VA. **Rig #3** was a tackle shop special. **Rig #4** shows Jack Stovall's buzz bait blade rig. **Rig #5** was Jim Walker's change—a smaller delta-shaped blade that has less water resistance. My small inline spinner blade decorates **Rig #6**. Spinner and buzz blades rotate better with two or three beads from the craft store (8 mm or so) in front of the blade. My wife insists on a brown and orange bead, buzz blade-combination.

All of these rigs are successful at times, although I think the flashy blades catch better. Rigs from **#4** through **#6** have a three-way swivel at the line end. The leader to our hooks goes on one swivel, the fishing line is attached to the second, and short mono dropper for a sinker is tied to the third swivel. Lately, I find that a short, solid connector is better for the sinker as it seems to tangle less.

Ultrasharp hooks tag more flounder. We use 1/0 Kahle lazer-sharpened hooks at leader's end. These hooks are nearly impossible to resharpen after denting them on a rock, but they will retain needle sharpness all day long in normal use. Unfortunately, their sharpness is due to being made of hardened steel, which is more prone to rusting.

Spreader rigs like those on the right are popular in some areas. The top spreader, made by Mai-Tai, has a 1/2-oz. ball sinker at the center of the spreader bar. The bottom two spreaders are my combinations of weights, delta buzz blades with bead "bearings." The bottom rig also has plastic tubing covering the .047" wire spreader.

While I have not experimented with any of these rigs for fish other than summer flounder, their fish-catching potential for bottom-feeding minnow-chasers could be limitless.

Spreader Rigs

How about trying them on other bottom-feeding game fish like walleye, sauger, perch, weakfish, sea bass—even catfish?

TYING BUCKTAIL HAIR ON A RIVET

A bunch of bucktail hair on a leader ahead of a minnow or other bait can be the additional attractor that makes the fish bite. One of the best ways to make such a sliding attractor is to tie the bucktail hair on a brass rivet—not a fun job. Disposable brass rivets are used to hold the parts of plumbing pipe compression fittings together until they are installed. The rivet spins around while you are trying to hold and tie on a hunk of loose bucktail hair. This makes for a lot of frustration, but is not insurmountable.

I found that a proper diameter punch that fits tightly inside the rivet, held in a vise, will make a suitable tying jig. Jam the rivet tightly against the punch's increasing diameter.

Wrap thread around the rivet as you would when making a bucktail jig, then apply a small hank of bucktail hair at a time, wrapping it with thread until you have enough hair on the rivet to cover it. Whip-finish the thread and seal it with epoxy or super glue. On the East Coast, some call this rig a "Flounder Pounder," where it is drifted along the bottom with various baits for flounder and seatrout. Favorite bucktail hair colors are white and chartreuse.

POLLOCK RIG FOR SHALLOW WATER FISH

Pollock Rig and Popping Plug with Two Treble Hooks.

Shallow water feeders like pollock, stripers, and blues often fall for popping plugs like the one on the right in the above photo.

At certain times of the year, however, those fish are feeding on smaller baitfish, about the size of the small bucktail jig leadered to the hookless plug on the left, called a "pollock rig." In use, the combo is cast out and the popper is worked as usual, with short jerks of the rod tip. When fish are attracted by the noisy presentation, they often hit the small bucktail. When brought to boatside, the hookless plug serves as a handle to hold the fish steady for netting or release.

Ray Hendrickson drills a tiny, shallow hole in the plug angled toward the rear to accommodate just the tip of the jig hook. The jig is hung in the tiny hole for casting, and improves distance. When cast, the combination has less wind resistance, and a shake or two of the rod tip will dislodge the jig for a normal retrieve.

See note on next page.

Note: Substitute a foam plastic popping cork for the hard-bodied popping plug described on page 169, and use a smaller jig on a similar leader to attract perch. Or, use a popping cork and a leader just long enough to keep a soft crab or baitfish above a grass bed on high water.

● ● ● ● ● ● ● ● ● ● ● ● ● ● ● ●

SOFT BAIT RIGS

Live baits like soft crabs and crawfish can be held on the hook with rubber bands or the elastic sewing thread found in fabric stores.

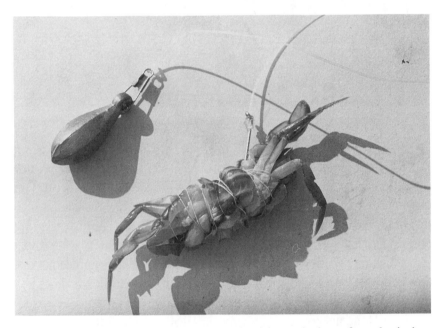

Large red drum are best tempted with a whole soft crab tied to a 7/0 hook with elastic sewing thread wound around the crab several times and tied off.

Old fishing books tell us that soft and papershell lobsters were also tied to hooks as striped bass baits along the Northeast Coast.

RIG TIPS

• As discussed in the "Knots" chapter, I get several feet of doubled line, sort of a "poor man's Bimini Knot" by tying my snap swivel on the end of a doubled line with a Palomar Knot, then using a Spider Hitch 2- to 3-feet up the line to keep the doubled line together. Yep, I said "snap swivel," which upsets bass anglers. I like to change lures frequently; try new goodies. That's part of the fun of fishing, right?

• An old tire chain, dragged slowly across the bottom at the end of a rope, can telegraph hard, rocky, or even oyster bottom, says Norm Haddaway. Finding oyster bottom is important for oyster tongers, and also points out fish habitat to anglers.

• Store your leadered flies, flounder rigs, or lures in zippered plastic bags labeled with a Sharpie® pen. Some anglers use pipe cleaners or twist ties around a coiled leader to keep it from tangling.

• When making up leaders, many toothy-fish anglers use a trace of wire at the lure to prevent cutoffs. Others have found a bite leader can be made from a short section of braided "superline."

The braided superline seems to have more resistance to sharp teeth than the fused type that sometimes frays at the business end.

• Form a loop with the running line, pass the loop through a sinker eye, then wrap a small rubber band tightly around the loop and sinker to temporarily secure it. When a fish hits, the sinker pulls out of the rubber band wrap for a tangle-free fight. You can also tie the sinker on with a weak thread so it will break in a fish fight.

• Tarpon anglers tie a cork float to the running line with weak thread—tarpon toss the cork in a minute. Don't use foam plastic packaging material as a float. It is not biodegradable and it is illegal to knowingly dispose of plastics at sea.

• Dipping the handles of wire-cutting pliers in liquid rubber makes them nonslip, even when your hands are slimy with fish gurry. Also, think about dipping sinkers in the same rubber coating to prevent dings in your boat's gel coat—the color might even attract fish!

• Lures rigged on leaders can be stored in out-of-date plastic 16 mm film cans found at yard sales like those on the left.

• In-line sinkers are often used in front of crankbaits to make them run deeper. Tie one sinker eye to the running line and the other eye to a 3- to 5-foot leader with a shallow-running crankbait at the other end so the lure will run above the grass.

• In-line sinkers used for drifting baits across the bottom usually have a 2- or 3-foot leader behind them. Make the leader of a lighter line test than the main line so it will break first in case of a snag. The same goes for trolling with a drop-sinker rig—the mono dropper should be 1/4 the test of your running line.

• Captain Jeff Shores (on the right) trolls seven umbrella rigs during the spring striped bass season in Chesapeake Bay. Each umbrella rig has eight hookless sassy shads trailing behind a heavy wire "X." Attached to the center of each umbrella rig is a longer leader with a heavy bucktail jig. Jeff has a way to keep these cumbersome rigs from tangling. He stores them in a waxed seafood box, separated by layers of heavy sheet plastic. One layer of plastic, one umbrella rig, etc., until 10 rigs are stored.

Umbrella Rigs like the one shown above are made of stainless steel wire with four outriggers that hold teaser lures to give the appearance of a school of bait. Only the center lure is armed.

• High-density foam plastic also makes a good place to store long leaders with hooks, flies, or jigs. A piece of 1-inch thick extruded polystyrene with several knife slits in each end for leaders makes a handy flounder rig storer. It keeps the leaders straight, too.

• Long leaders can be kept on a piece of PVC pipe, held in place with rubber bands as shown in above photo.

• Dr. Ed Hahn of Centreville, MD loosely wraps a nylon cable tie around a bundle of leadered hooks, and tightens the tie as hooks are removed.

• Feathered hooks with an egg sinker on the leader just ahead of the "lure" can be used in an emergency as a trolling temptation offshore or inshore.

• Tooth-defying, inexpensive lures for bluefish, king mackerel, and wahoo can be made from untwisted strands of polypropylene rope, wire-leader rigged with a 7/0 hook at the business end. Add an egg sinker at the head, or a strip bait at the tail end if desired.

• Sliding-sinker or "fishfinder" rigs can be made on the beach by hooking a bank or pyramid sinker in a snap swivel and threading the running line through its eye, then tying on a large swivel and a leadered hook. Substitute an egg sinker and have the same rig. A couple of beads between the sinker and the swivel will protect your knot.

• Enhance slow-trolled live or dead baits by adding a flasher spoon or a spinner blade and clevis ahead of the main attraction.

• Tie several #6 gold hooks on a 4- to 5-foot leader of 30-pound test mono with a sinker at the end and bait the hooks with a tiny piece of fish and you'll catch all the bottom-feeding baitfish you need for near-shore king mackerel and other gamefish.

• If you don't have cut bait for your multi-hooked bait-fish rig, tie a bit of bucktail or feathers on the hooks to imitate smaller baitfish.

• Small 1/4-inch diameter colored hoses armed with 1/0 hooks spaced 8 to 10 inches apart on a 30-pound test leader ended with a 4- to 6-oz. diamond jig will attract Atlantic mackerel by the cooler load. The macks are not only good to eat, but frozen chunks of mackerel are a great bluefish bait in the surf. Check out the spring schedule for Atlantic Ocean head boats. Take a big cooler.

• Frank Daignault ties a heavy metal jig into the leader ahead of a featherweight swimming plug for added casting distance—keeps the plug swimming a bit deeper, too.

• Tie a treble hook on the leader several feet ahead of a trolled swimming plug to catch and accumulate weeds.

• A quick Gypsy rig can be made by tying a three-way swivel to the end of the fishing line. The other two eyes of the swivel get different lengths of leader ended with lures of your choice.

• Craft shops are the usual places we find beads for our rigs. Think about buying cheap costume jewelry at yard sales for the same purpose.

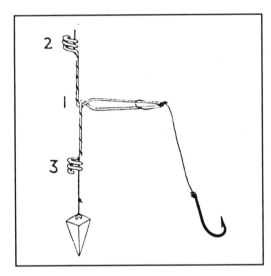

• Dave "Peanut" Sullivan of Berlin, MD developed the "Eastern Shore Quik Rig" on the left for surf and bottom fishing. Spaces between the top and bottom wire coils allow the angler to "wind" line or leader around without removing the sinker. "No knots, slippage, or line cutting," Peanut says.

• "Float-fishing" for king mackerel, we use the rig below, made from 6 feet of 40-pound test braided wire with a swivel and balloon float at one end and a three-way swivel at the other end. Two 1/0 stainless steel treble hooks on wire droppers complete the rig—both inserted in the live baitfish. Kings rarely miss both hooks.

• Balsa floats could be substituted for the balloons by using large rubber bands around the float to capture several passes of running line that release when the fish hits.

• Try a floating jighead behind or above a sinker when drift-fishing. It floats above the bottom, and since fish usually strike upward, it could gain you a few bites.

• A popular rig passed on by the (Chesapeake) Bay Country Bassmasters is a Carolina rig with an egg sinker ahead of two beads, then a swivel, a 2-foot leader followed by an air-impregnated salamander on a 5/0 worm hook.

• Ted Sheridan rigs a worm weight backwards ahead of a swivel stop, then ties on a 2-foot leader terminated by a worm hook and a green Mr. Wiffle®. "Deadly on spotted seatrout," Ted says.

• If you run out of brass sinker eyes when pouring up some large in-line or bell trolling sinkers, skin some #14 copper wire and wrap short sections of it around a finishing nail (head up) in a vise. Leave short "pigtails" to grip the lead inside the sinker.

• Bob Meushaw tied the above rigs for the feather jigs he made during the striped bass' heyday on Chesapeake Bay. When the stripers were feeding on silverside minnows, Bob lobbed this rig out (it can tangle when it is cast hard), and let it sink into a school of breaking fish. By whipping the rod tip, the feathered jigs "danced" around like escaping baitfish. Very effective!

• Downrigger weight tail fins can be bent to one side so they will run farther outboard when trolled, thereby keeping them apart on turns.

• Fly anglers often mark their lines with a Sharpie® pen where enough line has been stripped in for another cast. For night fishing, Tom Fote of Toms River, NJ overwraps the same place with fine thread and smooths it over with Pliobond®. When stripping in a fly at night, Tom can feel the proper "stop" as it passes through his fingers.

• A similar overwrap with a stopper bead below it serves a check for a sliding float to provide the proper depth for a bait. Make up a few of these knots on pieces of tubing and leave the ends long. After slipping the tubing to the proper spot on the fishing line, slip the knot off the tubing and pull the ends to tighten the knot.

• Jim Walker's rig for live-baiting stripers consists of a rotating hook standoff above a 6-oz. sinker. The swiveling standoff with beads above and below it will keep the rig from tangling. Its short-leadered hook holds a live spot or white perch. Very effective!

• Keep each different size of hook or snap swivel on a large snap swivel. Keeps down tackle box clutter.

• Loop-to-loop connections or swivels between leader and line won't go through the rod guides. Wind-on leaders allow the angler better fish control at boatside. Special splices are needed for wind-ons. Check with your local tackle shop for the proper tools.

• Wrap wire solder around a lure's hooks to make the plug run deeper, or to make a "floater" into a "submerger."

• Wear heavy leather welder's gloves when handling wire leaders with big fish attached.

The following pages include drawings of several basic knots, (courtesy of Stren® and Ande®) I have found helpful in my fishing. Here are a few guidelines, starting with line selection:

- Don't buy cheap line. Midpriced lines give the best performance for the dollar. Line is one of the cheapest items in fishing, don't skimp on quality.

- Practice tying knots. Start with a piece of clothes rope if that will help you to visualize how a certain knot will look when tied in a small-diameter line.

- Select lines for the use you intend to give them. For the type of fishing I do, it boils down to two types: Monofilament, and fused gel-spun polyesters—sometimes called "superlines."

- My personal preference is to use mono lines for almost all angling. I use the Improved Clinch Knot and the Uni-Knot for mono lines. Always moisten a mono line knot before tightening it.

- Manufacturers of "superlines" recommend the Palomar Knot for minimal slippage. Better yet, get the advantage of additional abrasion resistance by doubling 2 or 3 feet of line and tying a Palomar Knot at the snap swivel or lure, and a Spider Hitch 2 or 3 feet up the line.

- Always check the line for nicks or abrasions that will cause a weak spot. If you find abraded or nicked areas, check your rod guides to make sure they are not the culprit.

- Cut off 20 or 30 feet of line after fighting a big fish, and retie your knots.

- When it's time to change your fishing line, dispose of your old line in a safe, responsible manner. Never throw worn-out line overboard where it can create a fatal trap for fish and wildlife. Set an example for your companions.

- To learn more about knot tying and fishing line check the Bibliography for recommended reading and sources.

BASIC KNOTS

Blood Knot

The best knot for tying two lines together, of about the same diameter.

Improved Clinch Knot

Pass line through eye of hook, swivel, or lure. Double back and make five turns around the standing line. Hold coils in place, thread end of line through first loop above the eye, then through big loop, as shown.

Hold tag end and standing line while pulling up the coils. Make sure the coils are in a spiral, not lapping over each other. Slide tight against eye. Clip tag end.

Dropper Loop

This forms a loop in the middle of an otherwise knotted line, giving you a place to attach a hook, sinker, or fly. Though this is not a strong knot, it is useful with panfish and small saltwater species.

Form a loop in the line.

After eight to 10 turns, reach through
the center opening and pull the remaining
loop through. Keep your finger in this loop
so the loop will not spring back. Hold loop
with teeth and pull both ends of line,
making turns gather on either side of loop.

Set knot by pulling lines as tight as possible.
Tightening the coils will make loop stand out
perpendicular to the line.

Palomar Knot

1. Double about 4 inches of line and pass loop through eye.

2. Let hook hang loose and tie an overhand knot in doubled line. Avoid twisting the lines, and **don't tighten.**

3. Pull loop of line far enough to pass it over the hook, swivel, or lure. Make sure the loop passes completely over this attachment.

4. Pull both tag end and standing line to tighten. Clip tag end.

Perfection Loop

A perfection loop knot is used at the ends of the leader belly and the tippet.

A.

A. Double the end of the leader belly forming a loop about 6 inches long. Form a smaller loop about 2 inches from the end of the leader belly so that the smaller loop is behind the doubled line.

B.

B. With the larger loop, make a wrap around the smaller loop and pass the end of the larger loop through the smaller one

C.

C. Wet the knot area and firmly pull the larger loop. Be sure the wraps tighten evenly. Trim excess.

To connect the perfection loops, pass the tippet loop over the lure through the leader belly loop. Clip tag end.

Spider Hitch

This is a fast, easy knot to create a double-line leader. Under steady pressure it is equally strong, but does not have the resilience of the Bimini Twist under sharp impact. Not practical with lines above 30 pound-test.

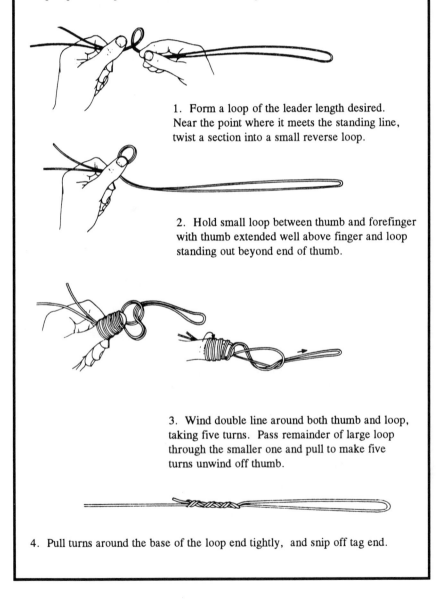

1. Form a loop of the leader length desired. Near the point where it meets the standing line, twist a section into a small reverse loop.

2. Hold small loop between thumb and forefinger with thumb extended well above finger and loop standing out beyond end of thumb.

3. Wind double line around both thumb and loop, taking five turns. Pass remainder of large loop through the smaller one and pull to make five turns unwind off thumb.

4. Pull turns around the base of the loop end tightly, and snip off tag end.

Surgeon's End Loop

Use this knot to tie a loop in the end of the line for attaching leaders or other terminal tackle quickly.

1. Double the end of line to form a loop, then tie an overhand knot at the base of the doubled line.

2. Leaving the loop open, bring the doubled line through once more.

3. Hold the standing line and tag end, and pull loop to tighten knot. You can adjust the loop size by shifting the loose knot before tightening. Clip tag end.

Surgeon's Knot

This knot joins a leader to a line. Unlike the Simplified Blood Knot, it effectively joins lines of varying diameters.

1. Lay line and leader parallel, overlapping six to eight inches.

2. Treating the two like a single line, tie an overhand knot, pulling the entire leader through the loop.

3. Leaving the loop of the overhand open, pull the tag ends of both the line and leader through again.

4. Hold both lines and both ends to pull knot tight. Clip ends close to avoid foul-ups in rod guides.

The Uni-Knot System

This system uses one basic knot for a variety of applications. The Uni-Knot can be varied to meet virtually every knot tying need in either fresh or saltwater. Developed by Vic Dunaway, editor of *Florida Sportsman* magazine and author of numerous fishing books including <u>The Complete Book of Baits, Rigs, & Tackle</u>. See Bibliography.

Tying to Terminal Tackle

1. Run line through eye of hook, swivel, or lure at least 6 inches; fold to make two parallel lines. Bring end of line back in a circle toward hook or lure.

2. Make six turns with tag end around the double line and through the circle. Pull standing line to slide knot up against eye. Tighten knot. Clip tag end.

Snelling a Hook

1. Thread line through hook eye about 6". Hold line against hook shank and form Uni-Knot circle.

2. Make 5 or 6 turns through loop and around line and shank as desired. Close knot by pulling on tag end of line.

3. Tighten by pulling standing line in one direction and hook in the other. Clip tag end.

ACCESSORIES————————————185

PIER CARTS

Pier fishing regulars use all sorts of wheeled vehicles to transport their tackle, coolers, lunch, bait, and sometimes even umbrellas, out on the longer piers.

On Maryland's Choptank River at Cambridge, two fishing piers were made when the center of an old bridge on Route 50 was removed. Fall fishing for sea trout is best at the far ends, near the channel—either 4,400-feet or 2,200-feet from your car—and walking to the far end of either pier with a load of gear is easier with a cart.

"I think it was a fantastic idea to make a fishing pier out of this old bridge," says Herbert Gough (below) who frequently fishes and crabs from the Fishing Piers at Cambridge.

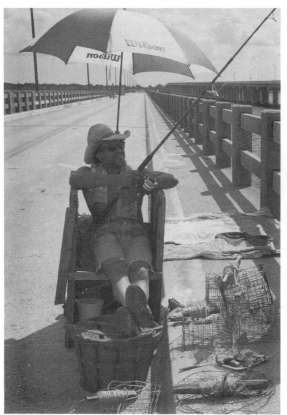

Gough has built himself a unique wheeled combination fishing tackle carrier/umbrella-shaded chair to transport his gear on his many Maryland fishing pier trips.

Grocery carts and little red wagons are often pressed into service to haul fishing gear onto piers like the Seagull Fishing Pier at the Chesapeake Bay Bridge-Tunnel across the mouth of Chesapeake Bay.

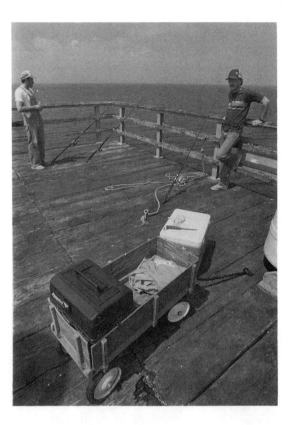

Fred Sharkey and Tom Goldston of Norfolk (above) fish the Seagull Fishing Pier. They spread their seven rods along the railing on the T-end of the Seagull Pier. "We catch good numbers of three-pound croaker here," Sharkey said, "and there are spot and gray trout aplenty in summer." Spring and fall see runs of monster bluefish pass the Seagull, and these anglers use a live spot floated under a balloon for the choppers. Sometimes a 40- or 50-pound cobia will hit the suspended spot.

Another suggestion for hauling fishing gear out on piers is a wheeled cooler for ice, tackle, food, and fish. One chap made a cart to tow behind his bike, allowing him to easily transport all the gear he needs.

I use a regular 2-wheel delivery dolly to carry tons of tackle and a huge ice-filled cooler down the dock to the boat. Beach anglers sometimes use a plastic child's snow sled—they attach a box to accommodate fishing necessities that has rod holders on each side.

Baitfish can be kept alive in laundry or peach baskets with a lid lowered in the water—or in white buckets with battery-powered fish aquarium aerators.

American ingenuity also comes into play in getting one's hooked fish from the water up onto the pier. Small fish are no problem to lift up to pier level. On lower piers, a long-handled gaff will hoist the biggest bluefish. But, on higher piers, regulars have designed hoop nets that can be lowered on parachute cord for medium-sized fish, and "bridge gaffs" made from giant lead-weighted treble hooks on stout cord are used to snag and raise bigger fish.

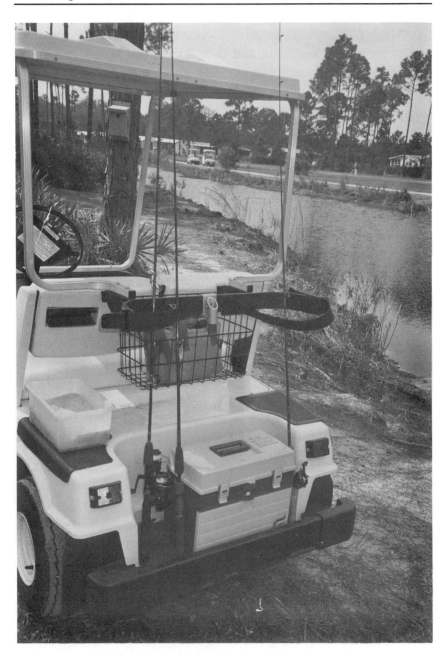

The author temporarily rigged this golf cart for bassin'.

RIG A GOLF CART FOR BASSIN'

Bass anglers who fish in lakes know their favorite fishing holes are just that—big holes in the ground, filled with water. So, it stands to reason that if someone digs holes in the ground, sooner or later they will fill with water and someone will stock bass in them.

Which leads us to golf courses; perhaps the largest untapped source of bass fishing anywhere. When bulldozers pile up all that earth to make greens, sand traps and the like, they leave a hole, or "borrow pit." When the pit fills with water, it becomes a "water hazard," an abomination to golfers, but when stocked with bass, it's the Promised Land to anglers.

Along every golf course, picturesque lakes and ponds provide pleasant scenery, water hazards to entertain golfers, and great habitat for bass and other stocked fish.

On a Florida golf course, I met Joe Anderson from Pennsylvania, who had a golf cart rigged just the way a non-golfing fisherman would want it. In place of golf bags on his cart, Anderson mounted fishing rod holders in back of the seat. A huge Phantom tackle box rode on the rear platform. Weather curtains and a radio for comfort. And, best of all, a trailer hitch. On a golf cart! Anderson had a small boat and trailer he moved around his favorite golf course from one (fishing) hole to another.

Golf etiquette dictates: "Wait until they play before moving up, and try not to make distracting motions or loud noises when a player gets ready to hit the ball."

We followed groups of golfers around the course in our bassin' cart until we saw a neat place to fish, then we stopped. We hid our carts behind bushes and behind the golfer's line of sight.

I see a fertile field to plow out there: Golf course managers opening up at 5 a.m. so anglers can fish the water hazards before the first golfer tees off. Bait and tackle in the Golf Pro Shop. Pro Bass Tours from course to course. Bass guides in golf carts. The new sport of golf cart bassin' is virtually untapped. Rig a golf cart for bassin' and go for it.

MAKE YOUR OWN SIDE PLANERS

Side planers, like outriggers and downriggers, can place the angler's lures in hard-to-get-at-places, or into shallower water than the boat engine will tolerate—and still allow the use of light tackle. They also get your lures away from the boat's wake.

My inexpensive side planer was made from 1 x 8 in. pine shelving and a few items from the hardware store. Two boards are required for each side planer. Mine are about 24" long, so an eight-foot board would make two complete planers, one each for port and starboard.

The first item of business is to cut off the front end of each 24" board at about a 20-degree angle, like the bow of a ship. The longest dimension will be the top of the planer when it is in the water.

Then, that cut must be beveled at about a 45-degree angle so the board will travel away from the boat. The beveled edge will always face toward the boat. Sit the board upright on its shortest edge and imagine how water pressure would act on the bevel, and you will see which side of the boat it will travel away from.

The unit we will make here is designed to run off the starboard side. If you make side planers for the port side, reverse the 45-degree bevel so the beveled edge faces toward the boat.

After your 20-degree angle and the 45-degree bevel cuts are made, offset the two boards about 7" and C-clamp them together (See photo on page 190, with the boards bottom edge up) on the workbench.

The next task is to mark, drill and place two 1-1/2" long 1/4"-20 stainless steel studs in the **bottom edge** of each board—for a total of four.

1. From the unbevelled end of the **protruding board** (rear board in the photo on page 190) measure 2" and strike a pencil line across both boards while clamped together.
2. Strike another line across both boards about 2" from the beveled edge of the **non-protruding board** (front board in the same photo).
3. Mark a 1" depth on a 1/4" drill bit with a piece of masking tape and drill holes 1" deep at the center of each board edge on your pencil lines.
4. Mix a small amount of epoxy and place a dab in each hole to secure a stud. Place a 1/4"- 20 Nylock nut on the tip of each stud to keep epoxy off the threads and place each stud about 1" deep in these holes.
5. Let the epoxy set up overnight.

Next day, with the boards still clamped together, turn them over and strike lines across them from edge to edge so the stud holes you have just made will line up with the stud holes you are about to drill in the opposite edge.

Repeat the marking, drilling, and setting of studs on the **top edge** of each board. Now you have four studs epoxied into the top edge of the boards, and four studs epoxied in the bottom edge.

While the epoxy sets up, cut four 12" long pieces of 1/8" x 3/4" aluminum or stainless steel bar stock. Drill a 5/16" hole 1/2" from the end of each piece of stock.

After the epoxy has set up, place two pre-drilled aluminum bars on the studs from the top edge of one board to the top edge of the other board, and two bars on the bottom edges of the boards as shown in the above photo. With the boards set on edge and their slanted ends in a position like the bow of a ship, place stainless steel 1/4"-20 wing nuts on the top studs, and 1/4"-20 Nylock nuts on the bottom studs. Snug the nuts down to allow only a slight amount of movement of the bars. The wing nuts are used to lock the unit in place folded flat for storage or opened up for use.

Next, drill a 1/4" hole about 4" down from the top edge and about 8" back from the "prow" of the outside surface of the board nearest to the boat (with the beveled edge nearest). Place a 1/4"-20 stainless nut and washer on a 6" eye bolt about halfway up, and put the eye bolt through the hole. Put a washer on the inside of the bolt, and run a 1/4"-20 Nylock nut down the threads until it is flush with the end of the threads. Then tighten the nut nearest the eye until the eye bolt is tight and snug.

Disassemble all your parts and place them in order of disassembly. Paint the boards with two coats of epoxy (I used West System®), allowing for drying between coats.

At this point, decide whether to apply a coat of blaze orange paint for visibility, or whether to mount a small blaze orange flag on top of each unit so people trolling near you can see the side planer. The final finish is up to you, but don't use the blaze orange spray that utility technicians use to mark buried power or phone lines under your lawn. That product washes off as you troll the unit in water. It is biodegradable. I know.

In use, 50 to 100 feet of parachute cord is tied to the eye bolt and connected to a midpoint on your boat. (Some anglers have a bow-mounted pole with two huge reels on it, one for each unit, port and starboard. Others simply tie the line to the after end of the bow rail as a temporary rig that can be easily removed).

When the sideriggers are deployed, the simple line-release device shown above can be used to carry your fishing line to the side planer and place your lure out of the engine's slipstream, or over shallow areas where your prop would be in serious jeopardy.

Make up several line release clips as in the above photo; each will include a shower curtain ring and a small alligator clip from the local electronics store, plus a 1/2" diameter circle of 1/8" sheet rubber or plastic. Cement or epoxy 1/2" disks of sheet rubber or plastic to each side of an alligator clip's jaws to hold your fishing line. Drill a hole in the clip's base to accommodate the shower curtain ring.

When trolling as in the above photo, if you have two sideriggers they are placed to port and starboard. When they are deployed, line release clips are clipped to the rod's line allowing 30 or so feet of line between clip and lure to make a "leader." Then, open the shower curtain ring and slip the line release clip over the line to the side planer. Let the clip slide down the parachute cord to the side planer. When a fish hits the lure the line is pulled out of the clip and the fish can be fought on light tackle.

It is not necessary to bring in the side planer each time a fish is caught. Simply re-clip the fishing line to another siderigger clip and send it down the parachute cord to the side planer again. A supply of release clips can be stored aboard for the possibility that you might find a mother lode of willing fish.

PLANERS AS DOWNRIGGERS

Planers are often used to take lures down to suitable depths. One problem with planers is they exert a lot of pressure on the tackle and one must use 30-pound gear or heavier to control even a medium-size lure/planer combination. When a fish strikes the lure on a leader behind the planer, the planer "trips" and relieves the downward pressure so the fish can be reeled in much easier.

Planers are effective, no question, but there is another way to use them so the angler can fight the fish on light tackle.

First, rig the planer on a heavy line; even clothesline will do, but parachute cord would be strong enough and its thinner diameter will cause less friction. Mark the line every 10 feet and keep track as you let the planer out, so you can repeat the depth if you get a strike.

Line release clips can be bought, or made from inexpensive parts as in the previous section about side planers.

Next, rig a line release in the aft hole of the planer. In use, the fishing line (light tackle is fine) is clipped in the release, and the reel's line sent down on the planer. When a fish strikes, as with a downrigger, the line snaps out of the release, and the fish can be fought on light tackle. A jerk on the planer line will trip it so it can be retrieved and reset.

DOCKSIDE FISH CLEANING TABLE

A five-gallon plastic bucket attached to a kitchen sink-cutout makes a good temporary fish cleaning table for your dock. Simply turn it upside down and place it over a dock piling and you're ready to filet fish. Remove it for storage if necessary. When we built our pier, the dock pilings were left at a convenient 32-inch height, above the decking, convenient for fish cleaning.

Kitchen sink cutouts already have a nice plastic laminate on a plywood base. I attached the bucket to the bottom of the cutout with four screws through the bottom of the bucket and spray-painted the bucket black to match the creosoted piling. Lath strips around the edge of the laminate top keep filets from slipping overboard.

Kitchen installers usually have the cutouts. Drywall contractors, bakeries, and farmers are a good source for surplus plastic buckets.

Left: The author installing his fish-cleaning table.

Right: Cleaning Fish

A CUP HOLDER FOR THE TOW CAR

Car cup holders are available from most auto supply stores, but I never found a size or configuration that suited my needs, or my vehicle. So, I made two of 5/16" plywood, one for my station wagon tow car and another for my wife's sedan.

Overall outside dimensions are: 9-7/8" long x 4-5/8" wide x 7-1/2" high. Each cup compartment is 4-3/8" square to contain the insulated plastic mugs so popular today—and there is a 1-1/4" wide handle slot that extends from the top to within 1/2" of the bottom of each cup compartment.

For rear-wheel drive cars with a "drive train hump" you can make a thin cardboard pattern to fit the round hump at the spot where the holder will be placed. This pattern will indicate the correct radius for the holder's bottom. Front-engine vehicles have either a small hump, or none at all. Adjust your bottom configuration accordingly to fit the floor.

I traced the tunnel hump pattern for my station wagon on the plywood, then measured and marked the wood for cutting the side pieces. Ends, separator, and the bottom were measured and cut.

The pieces of wood were squared up and joined with small finishing nails and glued joints. The unit was stained and varnished. I added a small detachable, compartmented plastic box (made for school lockers with a 3 x 3 in. sheet magnet attached) to the front side of the mug holder. Next, I glued a piece of sheet metal to the front side of the wood holder to attach the plastic box by its magnet. This attachment holds a vehicle log for business mileage, small notepad, pens, pencils, and a small calculator.

Fast or brake-jamming drivers can line the bottom curvature of the cup holder with hook-and-loop material to keep the unit in place in heavy stop-and-go traffic.

● ● ● ● ● ● ● ● ● ● ● ● ● ● ● ●

A SIMPLE FISHING TOWEL HANGER

Fishing towels seem to migrate around a boat, beach buggy, or out of a beach angler's pocket with some regularity. They're never around when you need them.

On my boat, fishing towels are held in place with plastic shower curtain rings. Plastic rings hold up better in the marine environment

and they don't leave rust marks on your boat's gel coat as do rings made of steel.

Simply punch a hole near one corner of a suitable fishing towel, or use a sewing machine to make a buttonhole on the towel, insert the shower curtain ring, then slip that ring around a bow rail, grab handle, cooler handle, surf belt, or any other convenient location.

Many advertising towels already have a brass grommet.

ROD HANDLE FISHBONKER

An embarrassing incident left a 15-inch-long piece of one-inch diameter hardwood trolling rod handle in my gunwale rod holder. Hefting the cleanly broken-off handle, it seemed that the handgrip was comfortable. If I added some lead to the broken end and a thong near the grip for safety I would have an inexpensive fishbonker.

I drilled a 9/16-inch hole about six inches up into the center of the broken end of the handle and made some rough angled holes inside the larger hole with a small drill bit to hold the poured lead in place.

Later, when I had the lead pot heated to pour some sinkers, I clamped the handle in a vise and filled the hole in the handle with molten lead. The trick here is to have the lead just hot enough so that it will pour, but not as hot as you would like it for making jigs or sinkers. If the lead is too hot, it will ignite the wood of the handle.

⚠ For safety when working with lead, always work in a well-ventilated area, and wear very heavy gloves so you won't burn your hands. The lead fumes can be toxic. Be careful pouring, too—a pocketful of hot lead can ruin your day.

Last, I drilled a 1/4-inch diameter hole through the grip end for a thong. Cotton cord could be wrapped around the handgrip.

My rod handle fishbonker is economical, easy to make, and is just the right size for pacifying medium-sized saltwater game fish like king mackerel and lunker bluefish.

FISH FLIPPER

Fish that are unpleasant or dangerous to handle with bare hands can be easily unhooked and flipped into the fish box or overboard with a simple buttonhook-like device. To make a "fish flipper," start with a 12-inch long piece of 1/8-inch or 5/32-inch diameter stainless steel rod and bend it so that a 1/2-inch deep and 1/2-inch wide hook is formed at one end of the rod. The stainless steel rod is bent by placing two 16 penny common nails vertically about 3/8-inch apart in a vise (with their heads, not their points, exposed for safety) to make a bending jig. Insert the rod between the nails about 3/4 of an inch and use the longer part of the rod for leverage to make the bend.

A handle at the other end of the rod can be as fancy or simple as needed. For those who have machining facilities, a fancy handle can be made from a four inch long piece of 5/8-inch diameter stainless steel bar stock which is then welded to the rod to form a "T" shaped handle, or drilled and tapped so the rod can be threaded and screwed into the handle.

A wooden handle can be made from a four-inch long piece of 1-1/4-inch diameter closet rod or dowel, as shown in the photograph above. Drill a hole through the dowel that is a neat fit for the rod, push the rod through the hole, then make a "U" shaped bend in the rod and drive the rod down into a shallow hole drilled into the top of the wood handle. If the rod is a little loose, a dab of epoxy will tighten it up.

In use, fish are flipped off the hook by grasping the flipper's handle in one hand and the hook's leader in the other (as shown in the drawings on page 202) and with the device's hook engaging the leader, the two are pulled away from each other until tight. When the flipper's hook engages the fish hook, the fish is given a rotary motion around the leader. The fish comes off the hook easily. The method works well for single fish hooks, but is not recommended for trebles.

When fish to be released are deeply hooked, there are several ways to get the hook out so the fish won't die. Most are based on the premise the hook can be backed out of a fish's gut, then retrieved through its mouth. Barbless hooks make this more feasible, but this advice also includes barbed hooks.

Another deep hook retriever is a long-nosed plier like the top item in the photo on page 200. Others include a flat piece of strap metal with a V-shaped notch in one end that engages the hook and forces it to back out of fish flesh, then engages the hook for easy removal.

My favorite is a Deep Throat Dehooker® (the bottom item in the photo on page 200) consisting of a 1/4-inch diameter piece of wire with a formed handle at one end and a "pigtail" at the other. The pigtail or curl is open enough to engage a hook leader and let it slide down to the hook, whereupon the angler jabs it slightly downward to back the hook out of fish flesh as shown in the drawings on page 202. The hook then "hides" in the pigtail so the angler can remove the hook from the fish's gullet. These are sold in fishing tackle shops.

Studies in Chesapeake Bay indicate deeply-hooked fish should have those hooks removed if at all possible to lower mortality.

DEHOOKER

(1) Hold the leader with your left hand and place the DEHOOKER around the leader with your right hand.

(2) Slide the DEHOOKER down the leader until it engages the hook.

(3) Pull the leader and the DEHOOKER apart.

(4) As you lower your left hand to the eight o'clock position, raise the DEHOOKER to the twelve o'clock position and gently shake the fish off without touching it.

DEEP THROAT DEHOOKER

(1) Hold the leader with your left hand. Place the DEEP THROAT DEHOOKER around the leader with your right hand, making sure the open end of the curl is facing you.

(2) Rotate the DEEP DEHOOKER clockwise 1/4 turn. The leader should now be in the center of the curl.

(3) Push the DEEP DEHOOKER down the taut leader into the fish's throat until it stops at the lodged hook. Raise the DEHOOKER until it is almost parallel to the leader.

(4) Thrust the DEEP DEHOOKER downward into the throat to disengage the hook. Retract the DEHOOKER and the hook so it will not re-engage and harm the fish.

MARKER BUOYS

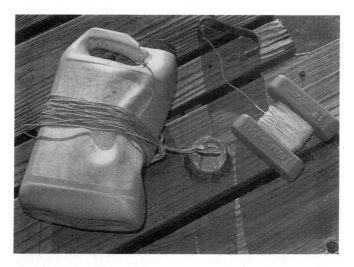

Buoys can be purchased to let us mark the spot where we find fish, wrecks, structure, or bottom contours. The "H-shaped" buoy on the right in the above photograph is a factory-made marker buoy. It is suitable for small waters, since its small size dictates it can only be seen for a short distance.

On big bodies of water like the Chesapeake Bay, a larger buoy is needed for good visibility. Even in rough water, a big jug can be hard to spot from a distance.

The one on the left in the photo was made from a one-gallon yellow antifreeze jug, about 60 feet of heavy twine, and an old duck decoy weight. The yellow jug is visible for long distances. Sixty feet of twine suits me, since I rarely fish in water more than 45 feet deep. Just about any heavy weight that will keep the jug in place would work.

Don't rely on someone else's jug to find you fish, though. Some rascals purposely toss their marker jug several hundred feet away from the action. (Refer to the double-buoy system on page 102 in "Anchoring" for another tip).

GPS and LORAN-C plotters may soon phase out the old reliable jug markers, but the jugs still work in a pinch.

COMBINATION LURE RETRIEVER/BOAT HOOK

A six-foot aluminum crab net handle was still in good shape when its wire netting rusted away. It was too good too toss out.

I made a combination lure retriever/boat hook from the net's aluminum handle, a brass snap, a screw eye, two wood plugs, two plastic furniture leg tips, and some epoxy.

First, I cut off two 2-inch pieces of wood dowel that fit neatly inside the aluminum handle. A pilot hole was drilled in one end of one wood dowel to accept the screw hook. A plastic tip was slipped over the handle and the screw hook was threaded into the wood.

⚠ For safety, round off the point of the hook with a file or grinder! Store it where the hook won't hurt anyone.

The other dowel was epoxied into the opposite end of the aluminum handle which was drilled out to accommodate the swivel end of the snap. Before the epoxy to anchor the snap set up, I slipped one plastic tip over the handle, then inserted the snap into the dowel.

To retrieve hung-up lures, clip the snap over the fishing line and slide it down the line to the lure. The depth at which a lure can be retrieved is limited by the length of the handle. When the snap reaches the hung lure, jiggle it around until the lure is free.

The opposite end of the combination tool can be used to grab dock lines and other boat-hook duties.

• • • • • • • • • • • • • • • •

CHUMMING GEAR

Chumming, the act of using all manner of fish food to attract fish to a baited hook, is used all over the world in freshwater and saltwater. Most common chum ingredients are mashed shellfish or ground fish, but also include veggies like corn and rice, macaroni, dog and cat food, and even pieces of whatever is being used for bait at the moment. There are many ways to deliver chum to the fish, some of which are illustrated in the chumming gear (CG) photo below.

Chumming Gear (CG).

An old meat grinder like the one at top center in the photo above can be found at a garage sale or flea market. In Florida and other locales where chumming is popular, large food grinders are mounted on boards and belt-driven by electric motors. Garbage disposal units have been used, but the danger here is that water and electricity are too close together, and such a unit should be rigged by an electrician. Large-scale (no pun intended) chum vendors use a garden chipper (honest!) which is incredibly dangerous.

Ground chum can be frozen, but just like bait, fresh is best. In the Chesapeake Bay and other areas, anglers often grind up fish carcasses after filleting the fish—then freeze the chum in 2" deep aluminum cake pans with slanted sides that will release the frozen block. This yields a flat chunk of chum which fits in laundry, onion, or citrus fruit bags (far left in the CG photo on page 205) tied to the boat's transom on the fishing grounds. As the frozen chum melts, it filters through the bag and forms a "chum slick" that attracts fish. Large mesh bags are best.

Another piece of equipment to hold chum is a 5-gallon plastic bucket with 1/2" holes drilled around the bottom third of the bucket to disburse the chum. Hang it off the transom—it will disburse the chum evenly. If you have a bucket minus the holes, use a ladle to distribute the chum, but you must maintain a solid chum line without breaks or you will lose the fish.

A minnow trap (top left in the CG photo), a cricket cage (center, with rope attached), or a homemade galvanized rat wire cage with a door, can be used to hold and disburse chum.

To make the PVC pipe chum pot (shown at the bottom of the CG photo), cut a 3-foot length of 4" diameter sewer drainfield pipe, drill several lines of 1/2" holes in it, and attach an end cap to one end with PVC cement. Then, drill a hole in the center of that end cap and one other end cap to accommodate a piece of bungee cord that acts to keep the unit closed after filling it. Make a loop on each end of the bungee cord: One for a sinker (or a sinker could be placed inside the unit), and the other loop for a line attached to your boat. These chum pots can also be attached to your anchor rode where it meets the anchor chain before anchoring, or hung from the transom. Dry, non-odorous chum can be purchased if the angler has an uneasy stomach.

Some might wonder why a can of cat food (shown under the grinder in the CG photo) is included. It makes great chum for bottom feeders like flounder, weakfish, croaker, and perhaps others in the freshwater realm that one might anchor to fish for. Buy the kind with a pull ring to open the can; attach a snap swivel to the ring, and add enough line to reach the bottom. Jim Walker of Bozman, MD says he outcaught some of the local good 'ol boys using this idea. He caught sea trout while they caught nothing. They all laughed—he ate trout that night.

To wrap up this chumming gear discussion, consider the chaps who use modified hair curlers as chum holders. (I'm not making this up. It was reported by esteemed outdoor writer Bill Burton in *The Capital* in Annapolis, MD). Hair-curler chum pots designed to upend and distribute their load of chum after they are shot with a slingshot to bait an area that will be fished. Look up this neat carp info on the Internet. Chumming technology has hit the carp-fishing world. What next?

● ● ● ● ● ● ● ● ● ● ● ● ●

ACCESSORY TIPS

• Place a strip of reflective tape on net handles, tackle boxes, and gaffs—or anything else you may want to find at night. Or, tape a flashlight to the net handle.

• Take the plastic tip off the end of your net handle and stuff the inside with foam packing peanuts. Tamp them in with a dowel. See if the net floats. It usually will.

• Handle toothy fish with crab tongs, available in areas where tidewater crabbing exists.

• Dr. Ed Hahn hangs a fly strip on the boat when biting flies are a problem.

• Carry one or two "Emergency Blankets" on the boat in cold weather. They are made from aluminized mylar first used on the Echo

Balloon in outer space, and reflect body heat back to the person wrapped in them. Usually available in camping or sporting goods stores.

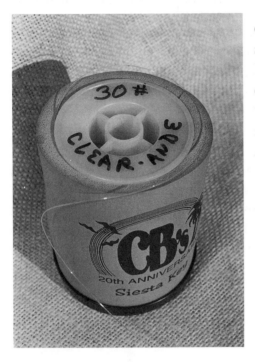

• Use a foam can cooler to store a 1/4-pound spool of fishing line as in the left photograph. The foam cooler keeps the line from unspooling, and out of the sun's injurious rays. I keep a spool of 30# test clear Ande® line on the boat for leaders, and to make up bottom rigs.

• Hang plastic grocery bags in your boat cabin for trash (hung outside they will blow away). Use plastic hooks with adhesive backing to hang the bags.

• An old shoelace or a piece of 100# test monofilament leader can be used to anchor your fishing hat in a breeze. Some anglers cut a length of mono line to fit around their neck and attach each end to both bows of their eyeglasses as a keeper.

• Keep spools of leader on a piece of bungee cord attached at each end to a convenient spot in your boat. Some anglers rig a plastic box to hold several spools of leader material by drilling holes in the side of the box and labeling the monofilament exit holes.

• On open boats in the winter, what I call a "basser's face mask" is a lifesaver The protector has a Velcro® brand strap that goes around the head and fits over glasses, caps, rain suits, etc. It is a great face shield in a fast boat. Called a *boater's vision visor* in bass fishing supply catalogs and costs about $20.

• Pouring outboard oil into a reservoir located inside the boat's hull can be messy. Use an antifreeze pourer available in auto parts stores for this task. It will have a twist-type shutoff valve and about 12" or so of clear plastic tubing. Mine exactly fits the screw top of a one-gallon plastic bottle of TC-W3® outboard oil.

• Stainless steel #11 crochet hooks can be used to pick out backlashes on reels. Just by having one aboard, you won't get backlashes, guaranteed.

• Big-water anglers often carry huge nets for large game fish they may want to release. In the Chesapeake Bay, they store these nets on top of the cabin. My tip? Anchor the net with bungee cord in rough water, or when running.

• Keep a balloon or two inflated and tied to a piece of monofilament long enough to reach bottom with a barbless hook on the other end. When a school fish like black drum is caught, hook the fish with the balloon rig and release it. Captain Buddy Harrison of Tilghman Island, MD follows a school of drum all day that way. Rubber balloons will biodegrade, styrofoam coffee cups will not. Consider the environment—'nuf said.

• Build your own minnow, eel, or crawfish trap from galvanized hardware cloth. Roll a 24 x 20 in. piece into an 8-inch diameter cylinder to make the unit, then make a funnel for each end. Use aluminum wire in freshwater to sew the cloth together, or use heavy mono line in saltwater.

• A tall plastic trash can is useful on a boat as a fly line stripping basket. Anchor the basket with bungee cord or a little water in the bottom, and leave 10 feet or so of fly line in it as a guide for the next retrieve.

• Grass shrimp are great baits for just about any saltwater game fish. They can be kept alive longer by building several "picture frames" of 1 x 1 in. stock and stapling plastic window screen to them. Grass shrimp are spread out on the screen, and the frames are stacked in a cooler until needed. Don't let water cover the shrimp.

• Keep sea worms and live eels from direct contact with freshwater or ice in the cooler with a plywood or foam plastic baffle.

BIBLIOGRAPHY

Dunaway, Vic, *The Complete Book of Baits, Rigs, and Tackle,* Wickstrom Publishers, Miami, FL. 1995.

Pfeiffer, C. Boyd, *Modern Tackle Craft.* Lyons & Burford, New York, NY. 1993. This 543-page compendium is the best reference for anyone who wants to make their own tackle.

TACKLE COMPONENT SUPPLIERS

(Check your local tackle shops first)!

Bass Pro Shops, 1-800-BASSPRO. Lure components, molds, hooks, accessories. Mainly freshwater related tackle.

Cabela's, 1-800-237-4444. Rod and lure making supplies, fly tying, etc.

Jann's/Netcraft, Orders only number 1-800-NETCRAFT. Information number 1-419-868-8288. Rod, lure, fly tying supplies, and books. Molds, accessories, tools, etc.

Offshore Angler, 1-800-4-OFFSHORE. Saltwater rigging materials and tools. Baitwells, etc., plus offshore accessories.

Orvis, 1-800-548-9548. Fly tying materials and tools, accessories, and fishing tackle.

BOAT & FISHING SUPPLIES

Boat/U.S., 1-800-937-2628. Boat accessories and fishing tackle. Retail stores nationwide, plus catalog sales. Memberships available.

Boater's World, 1-800-826-2628. Boat accessories and fishing tackle. At this time, 87 retail stores nationwide, plus catalog sales.

West Marine/E&B Discount Marine, 1-800-BOATING. Boat accessories and tackle. At this time, over 200 retail stores nationwide, plus catalog sales.

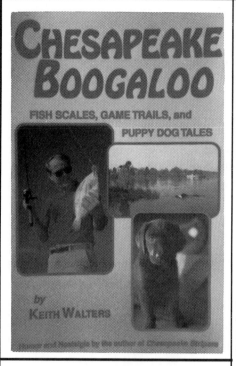

ISBN 0-9627039-1-5

Soft Cover 6 X 9, 224 pages

66 Photos + Drawings

Retail Price $17.95

Autographed Copies Upon Request

"Full of laughs (and a few tears). This book is a major (and will be a lasting) contribution to the region's literature... leaves the reader feeling as if there should be more, more, more..."
...... *Mason-Dixon Line*

" Delightfully offbeat Bay adventures..."
......*New Bay Times*

WHAT REVIEWERS SAID:

"A tear came to my eye..."
.....*a Chesapeake angler*

"Author Keith Walters boogaloos his way to a third book ....stories about snallygasters, toadfish tournaments, head fish, doublers, rockfish, peculiar hunt clubs, and a bewildering array of the author's offbeat outdoors companions."
.....*Easton Star-Democrat*

"It's a light, humorous read, one that will evoke your own memories of fishing trips, special friends, and exceptional dogs."
.....*Eastern Shore News*

"An outdoorsy dance around Chesapeake Bay, a happy time, a gathering of the author's favorite hunting, fishing, and Labrador retriever stories told in an entertaining fictional style."
.....*Newsday*

"It's about fishing, hunting, and rambling in the Chesapeake Bay region."
.....*Virginia Afield*

"Peculiar outdoor clubs, dogs with an attitude, and toadfish tournaments are a few of the subjects covered. Walters says some adventures really happened but are recounted in a fictional style. Others are mostly fiction presented as fact ("Something all anglers understand," he says)."
.....*Chesapeake Bay Magazine*

"Keith's fabulous story telling places you smack dab in the middle of interesting, unusual and hilarious events (oodles of them)..."
.......*The Fisherman*

Aerie House   **BOOK ORDER FORM**
P. O. Box 279
Bozman, MD 21612-0279
410-745-2236

SPECIAL OFFER
AERIE HOUSE WILL PAY FOR SHIPPING TO ONE ADDRESS ON
PREPAID ORDERS OF 2 OR MORE BOOKS (ANY COMBINATION).

Author's Signature Only___ Personalized w/names for gift giving?
___yes ___ no. Please specify below which book(s) you want autographed.
Should we enclose a gift card stating the book is from you? __Yes __No

(Please Print Names)   **Book Title**

_____   _____

_____   _____

ANGLER'S WORKBENCH
    Number of copies _____ @ $17.95 $ _____
    Maryland residents add $ .90 sales tax per book   _____
    Shipping add $1.65 per book   _____

CATCHING STRIPED BASS
    Number of copies _____ @ $3.95 each $ _____
    Maryland residents add $.20 per book sales tax   _____
    Shipping add $1.10 per book   _____

CHESAPEAKE BOOGALOO
    Number of copies _____ @ $17.95 each $ _____
    Maryland residents add $ .90 sales tax per book   _____
    Shipping add $1.65 per book   _____

CHESAPEAKE STRIPERS
    Number of copies _____ @ $19.95 $ _____
    Maryland residents add $1.00 sales tax per book   _____
    Shipping add $2.05 per book   _____
                 TOTAL ENCLOSED $ _____

MAIL ORDERS ONLY!
Make Checks or Money Orders Payable to Aerie House.
Send to: Aerie House. P. O. Box 279, Bozman, MD 21612-0279

SHIP BOOKS TO: (Please Print)————————————————
STREET: ——————————————————————————
APT. NO. ——————————— **P. O. BOX NO.** ——————————
CITY:————————————————**STATE:** ——— **ZIP CODE:** ———
PHONE #: (In case we have a ? about your order)—————————————
This page may be photocopied.

Aerie House is a division of Keith Walters LLC.